Richard ShadowFox

TAROT
of the
NIGHT

4880 Lower Valley Road • Atglen, PA 19310

Other Schiffer Titles By the Author:

ShadowFox Tarot
(with Jennifer ShadowFox)
ISBN: 978-0-7643-3487-0 $29.99

Tarot Deck of Heroes
ISBN: 978-0-7643-4024-6 $24.99

Copyright © 2013
by Richard ShadowFox
Library of Congress
Control Number: 2013946906

All rights reserved. No part of this work may be reproduced or used in any form or by any means—graphic, electronic, or mechanical, including photocopying or information storage and retrieval systems—without written permission from the publisher.

The scanning, uploading and distribution of this book or any part thereof via the Internet or via any other means without the permission of the publisher is illegal and punishable by law. Please purchase only authorized editions and do not participate in or encourage the electronic piracy of copyrighted materials.

"Schiffer," "Schiffer Publishing, Ltd. & Design," and the "Design of pen and inkwell" are registered trademarks of Schiffer Publishing, Ltd.

Designed by Justin Watkinson
Type set in CaslonOpnface BT/ NewBskvll BT
ISBN: 978-0-7643-4551-7
Printed in China

Schiffer Books are available at special discounts for bulk purchases for sales promotions or premiums. Special editions, including personalized covers, corporate imprints, and excerpts can be created in large quantities for special needs. For more information contact the publisher:

Published by
Schiffer Publishing, Ltd.
4880 Lower Valley Road
Atglen, PA 19310
Phone: (610) 593-1777
Fax: (610) 593-2002
E-mail: Info@schifferbooks.com

For the largest selection of fine reference books on this and related subjects, please visit our website at **www.schifferbooks.com.**

We are always looking for people to write books on new and related subjects. If you have an idea for a book, please contact us at proposals@schifferbooks.com.

This book may be purchased from the publisher.
Please try your bookstore first.
You may write for a free catalog.

Dedication

To things that go bump in the night!

And
Pamela Colman Smith

The image of the Hermit
is dedicated to my lighthouse in the storm
Donnaleigh de LaRose

Acknowledgments

A special thanks to my friends
Mary Nale
Cheryl Lynne Bradley
and
My editor, Dinah Roseberry
My publisher, Pete Schiffer
Stacey McNutt & Heidi McCauley
The entire staff of Schiffer Publishing

Introduction	5
The Tarot Cards	9
Major Arcana	10
Minor Arcana	74
Swords	74
Wands	104
Cups	134
Pentacles	164
Court	194
Swords	195
Wands	207
Cups	219
Pentacles	231
Tarot Spreads	243
Three Card	244
Celtic Cross	245
Vincit Omnia Veritas	247
Doing a Reading with the Vincit Omnia Veritas	249
When All is Said and Done	254

There is something about the night that makes our world different, other than the obvious lack of natural light of course. The affects are more personal and internal, as darkness takes away vision and triggers a keen awareness in the other senses. At the same time, our imagination, usually reserved for envisioning the future, becomes focused on the present moment. With all due respect to Descartes, we sense therefore we are, and we think therefore we will be.

The ability to think in the form of imagination allows us to envision a future, and make a plan to make it a reality. Our senses tell us where we are, and our imagination shows us where we want to be in the future. From that perspective our imagination is similar to, but so much more than, just a sense, because it allows us to go beyond the basics of finding food and shelter, or in other words, simple existence.

There isn't any mystery in how we discover our environment through the five senses, but we process so much information simultaneously from them that our mind filters and prioritizes, limiting our conscious awareness. That essentially means that we have information we don't know we have, and in turn it indicates that our own minds are capable of deciding what we need to know, without asking us first.

Now suppose a thought, perhaps in the form of an idea, appears in your mind. Who is to say that your mind is telling you everything? It might, for example, be omitting the source. I am not intending to diminish originality and creativity, but instead describing how we are all certain to have another information interface, a sixth sense, and that our own minds do not need to reveal it to us to make it a fact.

Introduction

At night, in the darkness, our imagination takes over for the lack of visual input, and the source of a simple sound is visually created within the mind. The epinephrine flows, and although there is fear, it is a euphoric fear. We like it and want more, all because our imaginations took over for our eyes.

As a young child, one of my favorite things was a quick game of hide-and-seek with my mother at bedtime, just the two of us. I would count while she would hide somewhere inside our modest two-story house. My excitement grew as I would peer around every corner and open every closet door. When I would inevitably find her, I would squeal with laughter as she popped out of her hiding place and said *boo*. Even though I was certain I would eventually find her – and the suspense revolved around only when, not if – it was thrilling, and I loved every second of the game.

Roller coasters, fictional haunted houses, and horror movies are examples of how we seek this feeling in controlled environments, and because of our imagination, we can still enjoy fear in situations with minimal risk. Yet how does this work, since we are actually safer in the aforementioned environments than in a car, and we hardly give the car a second thought? Yes, an imminent threat is the key, but in fictional environments, it is immanent instead; the mind is tricking us by engaging the imagination, and it is entertaining.

You Had Me at Boo

Then there is the spirit world, ghosts that roam and tease of their existence, never offering proof. On occasion, our imagination can create them, but what if there is a specific reason why that happens? What if, as I alluded to before, the imagination is the interface of the sixth sense. The overall definition of the word *imagination*, which I have paraphrased here, is, in the mind, outside direct influence of the five senses, and this is completely consistent with what I am describing.

Of the nonfiction variety, we can find ships, trains, hotels, and all kinds of buildings, cemeteries or ever-popular haunted houses where things are going bump in the night. In this era, you can even define ghost hunting as a science, but the spirit world wonderfully remains controversial and unproven. There is a tendency by some people to see things that are unable to be proven true as automatically false. Then those who see things that are not proven to be false as being possibly true, are labeled as fringe or worse. That unbalanced approach hardly seems fair at all.

Having faith means that one believes in things that offer no proof to substantiate the belief, and if one follows the mainstream or the masses, then it is perfectly acceptable. However, if one points their faith in a slightly different direction, it is not faith anymore, it is foolishness. Therefore, I am a fool, and perhaps that is a fact. So be it. I have had a number of experiences in my life that give rise to the possibility that aspects of this Universe are beyond our known scientific comprehension.

I embrace and have faith in what is described as the mystical because I have had intuitive thoughts, or feelings, that became actualized. This is not me claiming to be a prophet, or even psychic; I merely correctly anticipated future events. I did not have actual visions or dreams, only feelings I refused to dismiss.

If you are familiar with me and any of my previous work, then you should know that I am true to one source, one entity of inspiration, Pamela Colman Smith. I consider her to be a special friend, and no, we don't get together, sit around, and talk. She doesn't roam my halls with a lantern or appear to me in the reflection of a window. What I am confessing to here, is that I have no conscious perception of where my ideas come from when I create an image for a card. Does it come from my imagination? Okay, but again, what is imagination?

I believe that in my case at least, it is otherworldly, and that makes it something for which I do not wish to take credit. When I have intuitive experiences, I do not actually go to the future to get information; someone or something brings it to me in the present.

Since I accept the concept that I can be given a thought, or feeling, for the purpose of anticipation, it is completely consistent for me to believe that is also the source of what is referred to as my imagination.

Perhaps it seems arrogant for me to say that such a legendary Tarot artist as Pamela Colman Smith would choose me of all people to inspire, but then again maybe I chose her. I studied her iconic Tarot deck through a magnifying glass and wanted to understand her every choice of subject, environment, object, and color. I was reaching out to her and I believe she responded and willingly inspires me. If anyone has a powerful passion, a love for doing something that is strong, then it will reach the Magicians that exist for all of us, and inspire us through our imagination.

What's a Little Haunting Among Friends?

The Tarot Cards

Fool

UPRIGHT

Life is an adventure, as just being alive is a risk in itself, and the interpretation here is not why, but why not, when an opportunity of desire presents itself to you. This is not a card representative of definitive change in the sense that something will end so something else can begin, as there are many journeys, and they often overlap.

The possibility that one has encountered a fork in the road is there, but when this card appears in a reading, it should also be considered that one's path might have expanded to include someone or something new. The decisions one makes are the navigational mechanism of the path, and this should not cause a revelation in one's thinking.

The foolishness of one's choices belongs to the perception of others, and even if there is validity in the sentiment, it is still limited. The value and risk can only be understood and determined by the one facing the choice, well-meaning advice notwithstanding. The appearance of this card should not be confused with rash or irrational choices. Spur-of-the-moment, spontaneous actions, driven by feelings, are not inherently bad ideas, even if others may think that they are when offering advice.

An important aspect of this card is a positive – not negative, not ambivalent – approach to what lies ahead. If one looks to coincidence when an opportunity presents itself along their path, then there must not have been any prior expectation of purpose. The path defines the opportunity; the opportunity does not define the path, or it shouldn't, unless one is hoping to bounce from one lucky break to another.

A positive, if not enthusiastic attitude brings confidence, and although it doesn't eliminate risk, it gives value to weigh against the risk. That is how foolishness is removed from one's choices, and why others who do not desire as one does, think or feel, as one does, cannot make one's choices for them.

REVERSED

With enough thought, we can talk ourselves out of any good idea that comes along, and we often go against our feelings because of fear – a fear based on experience, or just being frightened of the unknown. One possibility this card represents reversed is letting the fear block the right choice. Rational thinking is of course prudent, but here we often have the rationalizing of an irrational decision. It is not defined here, which is the *right* choice, as that should actually be determined by looking to the why or why not when making the decision. This can apply to any choice, including the choice not to decide.

The best interpretation here relates to what happened, or did not happen, before the current situation. If one is not prepared, the ability to make a decision may be overwhelmed by emotion, and since emotions are reactions, they are likely to inappropriately influence a decision when it is unexpected. To understand emotions, and why they are always reactive, both positive and negative, one simply needs to examine the point in time in which they appeared. Everybody is different in respect to how they react, respond, and reveal their emotions, but that does not diminish my assertion. The difference maker in decision-making is quite often the internal emotional influence.

By no means am I stating one should not follow their heart and feelings, but they should not follow them over a cliff either. Evaluating a situation with one's mental ability to reason, and as a result determining how much influence they are allowing their emotions to have, won't take the fun out of a rational feeling; it will enhance it with confidence and trust.

At the same time, an irrational feeling will be exposed and the possibility of an even greater and further damaging emotional reaction in the future can be reduced. The path of life is a concatenation of events and every link carries forward emotionally and thoughtfully, while shaping future decision-making. The presence of this card reversed represents a need to take a closer look at that influence.

Magician

UPRIGHT

What stands out here is that each one of us has an ability, a talent, perhaps currently hidden, that when properly cultivated allows us to achieve and excel. It is not always obvious, and it may not be easy to find and develop as the influence of others can often lead one off the path.

The elements of this card point toward a gift bestowed upon each of us as individuals, but it requires persistent desire in the form of wanting it bad enough to overcome resistance and honor one's own commitment to make it a reality. Nothing worth having is ever easy. Okay, I said it. I didn't want to, but I did anyway. The reason for my dilemma is the word *having*: it really doesn't tell the whole truth. I prefer, nothing worth *being* is ever easy. Passionate feelings and strong desires are not reserved for, and certainly are not limited to, love interests. When one observes people who are fulfilled by their craft, they have succeeded by their commitment and drive, and what one must come to understand and accept is that we do not aim our passions, our passions aim us.

Expanding on that, we never choose to like something, or someone; we make a choice because we like it, or them, first. As I have said, our emotions are reactions, and we are drawn toward that which causes positive emotional responses. If one chooses to try something new, their emotional reaction will determine if they want to experience it again. One's feelings are positive and negative reinforcement, and their purpose is to draw us in the right direction.

It is not my intention to explain away the power of feelings as mere control devices, in effect unromanticizing them, but instead I wish to prompt one to follow their heart, the direction their feelings are leading them, to even more and greater positive feelings.

Other elements to consider when this card appears are creativity and initiating new activities that further one's progress toward their goal. A unique aspect of this card is that it is among the few outside of the Court that can be designated as a Significator, or a representation of an individual when it is found in a reading.

In that regard, it is viewed as a mentor or a person of substantial positive influence upon one, perhaps an idol or iconic figure.

REVERSED

Is the ability to deceive, trick, or con others, a gift to be utilized to achieve fulfillment? It is emphatically not, and when reversed, this card represents just that. Borne of disingenuous thinking, this is a perversion of an ability that one has embraced for the sake of traveling an easier path, and/or lowering others to make themselves appear more significant. Whether it is a single act of deception to advance an effort toward a goal, or a lifestyle, it leaves tragic results in its wake. The purpose of a gift is to provide one an ability to raise themselves to greater heights for personal fulfillment and the benefit of others, not for self-gratification at the expense of others.

We learn many things as we grow up, but what we learn about ourselves is at the heart of who we are now, or will be in the future. If one learns that others will trust, then when one deceives them, then one is focusing on the weaknesses of others for the purpose of exploitation, and completely ignoring what one is learning about themselves.

Being deceitful for protection from punishment, and to gain unearned rewards becomes a behavioral pattern that will in the end betray the deceiver. There is no true fulfillment provided by the intentional disregard, or abuse of another's trust. The primary interpretation of this card when found reversed is deception, exploited trust, and the inappropriate use of ability, to achieve selfish-minded goals. How we deal with the obstacles in our path is what defines us.

This is a reminder that each of our paths intersects the paths of others, and if we take a selfish approach to these intersections, we will not find fulfillment. If one encounters an obstacle, of a human nature, there will be no benefit in attempting to out-deceive them, as the word overcoming is not just meant as getting beyond, it is literal in a behavioral sense.

High Priestess

UPRIGHT

This is another card that can represent someone in a reading, or be chosen as a Significator beforehand. It can describe wisdom and psych acuity, the keeper of esoteric knowledge, but this might be misleading. True wisdom understands that esoteric does not mean a wall without passage, and the representation in this card refers to the gate, or gatekeeper. What is missed, and the message often found here, is not to focus on the wall, but for one to open their mind and focus on the knowledge within. It is accessible to anyone, and the wall that keeps one out is a self-imposed illusion.

Breaking apart the overall, such elements as getting in touch with oneself, and being open to intuitive and creative inspiration, may apply to the current situation. As cliché as it sounds, getting in touch with oneself is essential to defining and following one's path. If one knows who they are, does that automatically mean they know who they are not?

Thoughtful decisions require, you guessed it, thinking about the choices. However, does the decision shape who one is, or instead, does the understanding of who one is shape the decision. The choices one makes will influence what others may think about them, but that shouldn't apply to one's own understanding or perception.

The word psychic by definition refers to the mind, not the physical, and specifically relates to sensitivity to nonphysical influences or forces. Personally, I believe that the mainstream assertion that our minds consist of nothing but storage, a processor, and five interfaces is actually ironic. One need only think of the possibility, whether accepting or dismissing, to realize the five senses alone could not lead us to even consider there might be a sixth interface. In other words, what is the origin of the concept if our minds are that limited? Included in the interpretation of this card is a need to be open-minded and receptive to psychic influences, and I believe that it is there and available to anyone who is open to its guidance.

REVERSED

A possibility in this card reversed is someone has a habit of pretending to know something they clearly do not. Wisdom never describes all knowing; it is the ongoing process of learning based on the acceptance and humility of what one does not know.

This also may represent skepticism on matters of the occult or psychic abilities. There are parallels in these possibilities in that they both may describe a resistance, whether it is terrestrially provided knowledge, or a revelation of thought that enters the mind from something other than the five known senses.

One aspect found here is that the opinion or information provided is proven because the provider believes it to be true. Whether arguing against facts or taking one side of a philosophical divide, stubbornly insisting someone align their beliefs in accordance with the presenter is egotism, and is at the heart of the interpretation of this card.

History has shown that tragedy is often the result of conflict that escalated over a difference of opinion, where influence became a demand that would not relent until capitulation. It does not have to be on a global or regional level to be harmful; any two people can travel the same tragic path.

This card reversed can specifically reflect skepticism, a resistance, or doubt, on matters of the occult and psychic abilities, and it can be the primary interpretation here. Holding to the contention that one's belief does not ensure truth, there is still a spiritual or psychic reference in this card upright and reversed. One can and should decide on their own what that means to them, but it should be considered and evaluated upon the presence of this card in a reading.

Being open-minded is not a fault or weakness, and a willingness to think in terms of possibilities does not constitute acceptance of them. Standing on one side of a belief out of fear of ridicule is relinquishing control of your choices, and letting others define you.

Empress

UPRIGHT

An unmistakable, an undeniable mother exists for all that exists, and this is represented here. Motherhood encompasses so much more than birth, as the nurturing of life is just as vitally important to its existence. That element draws in all of humanity, man and woman alike, in the caring of the life that we live upon, and all life of this Earth. If we act appropriately life will flourish and our environment we live in will be lush and fruitful. This is to be celebrated as the most powerful gift ever given, and it is to be admired, respected; never taken for granted.

Every one of us has one, many of you are one, and I cannot imagine what could be a more significant ability. An opportunity to become the essence of the mother is represented here. What that truly entails is boundless in its interpretation, but it really is a matter of recognizing the point of need.

This very book is the child of the mother of creation. It had to be nurtured as anything is, and its acceptance will likely rest upon how I embraced that responsibility.

The question to ask, is if the mother can in and of itself be self-serving. The answer can be lost in the timeline of purpose, because the reward is often far in the distance. Found in pride after a long laborious journey, the essence of life, whether it breathes, or is the object you now hold in your hands, it is diverse in its nature, but emphatically it has an origin and a need to be nurtured into existence. The mother is for all intent and purposes the first in everything; there simply is nothing without her. To embrace her presence and recognize her purpose is where what matters most always begins.

REVERSED

The greatest obstacles we face often begin with denial. The denial of one's abilities, the denial of one's responsibilities, or the denial of purpose, are all the same on the surface. Underneath however, is the effect it has on you or those around you.

The unwillingness to proceed out of fear of failure is one possibility, and choices made out of fear will not result in progress. Another possible interpretation here is the corruption of power. If given a gift and recognizing it in the form of desire or potential, then one must consider the purpose behind their choice, and if one seizes the authority provided by motherhood with self-serving demands, then one is dismissing the free will of another.

The difference between what one can do and what one should do weighs heavily on my philosophy, and it would be contradictory for me to impose that line of thinking on another. However, what one has to consider for themselves is the same; can I, should I, why or why not, are the questions often not asked of oneself in this situation.

A gift, ability, or a position of authority, bring with them a responsibility. What is that responsibility and to whom it is due, is the reality behind the appearance of this card reversed. Denial can be a comfortable and safe place to live, but it truly impedes progress. Understanding why one chooses the way they do is a thread that runs through the Tarot, and if one is in denial of being in denial, then evaluating one's choices will likely be fruitless; with responsibility having been deflected.

Emperor

UPRIGHT

Authority provides comfort in security and structure, and it is really is something that we cannot live without. There are those who naturally project it, and those who naturally follow it, and each compliments each other.

The most tragic misconception, and it is easily recognizable, is the inverted thinking that purpose serves the authority, when in fact the reverse is true. The true essence of authority lies solely in one's responsibility to others, and how that authority serves the purpose at hand is the key element.

As well as the authority element of this card, the father aspect may also be present, and one does not exclude the other. Providing leadership to others and properly influencing a child both require the same approach. In a single sentence; offering guidance and support in the pursuit of goals. Proper authority requires strength, but that is strength of character and includes patient resolve. This card has the ability to represent a person, or the behaviors equated with the meaning.

When it appears upright it may represent an opportunity, a purpose, or perhaps serve as a warning to maintain a proper perspective. To play the role of the father one must guide and assist authoritatively, but with compassion, understanding, and patience. There is no other way.

REVERSED

The abuse of authority is common in our world, and often seems quite obvious if one is of the right perspective. There are times where borderline, and even emphatic disregard, can be hidden behind such extenuating descriptions as management style or strong leader. There are always cases where a firmer authority is necessary, but the two descriptions, style and strong do not define any versatility in approach. Practicing authority is not a "one size fits all" proposition; it cannot be inflexible. The reversed interpretation of this card can be anything from inability to understand up to blatant disregard, and anything in between.

Our experiences in life give us a personal perspective of fair leadership and this can possibly be improperly tainted. From that, in the context of a reading, with this card in a position associated with the querent, it is possible that a matter of personal perspective is affecting a view of authority. A quite familiar example would be the teenager finding themselves grounded for missing curfew and exclaiming, "That is so not fair!" Taking into account that from that simple example, we truly don't know if the punishment fits the crime, but we do know that personal perspective will always play a role.

Authority often does seem to translate into a sword to wield, and this card reversed is describing the abuse of that power, albeit, person, behavior, or perspective. It is really a matter of evaluating one's own perspective in any case before judgment is passed on another or situation, then acting accordingly.

Hierophant

UPRIGHT

In its simplest form, we have a standard or a foundation for belief in this card. However, very few things are really that simple when your quest is for answers to important questions. A dogmatic structure is rigid and unyielding, whether it be religion, academia, or merely traditional. It often amounts to doing something, and doing it a certain way, because that is the way it has always been done.

In every case it is of terrestrial origin, but quite often it is presented and enforced by an Earthly advocate on behalf of a celestial entity. It isn't limited to religion; however, that is a very common interpretation for this card in a reading.

We are all very familiar with rules, and in most cases we can see the logic that led to their origins. Then there are some rules that are implemented to exercise control over others. This doesn't make these rules malicious or harmful, but it also doesn't make conformity to them an insignificant decision to make. Additionally, there are many written and unwritten codes of conduct mandated by authority in every organization. Understanding the intent behind the circumstance, and evaluating one's options is a primary consideration.

When do we have the ability to make a different choice? This could be at the heart of this card's appearance. It could possibly represent a dogmatic authority personified, an institution or its rules, or just the mores themselves. There will be or has been involvement on some level with one of the aforementioned elements.

There is neither an inherent good nor bad here, as that choice comes within context. Rules defeat chaos and anarchy, and are one of the primary requirements to managing a civilization. How one is affected by this aspect of society on an individual basis is the usual application here.

REVERSED

With authority comes power, and the tools of power are rules and influence. In the human condition of self-awareness, the fueling and diminishing of the ego is of paramount importance to each of us. The ability to make decisions for others fuels the ego and this can translate into arrogance, narcissism, and a need to feel the power by exercising authority. This can taint the implementation of rules and is the abuse of authority that may be reflected here.

The paths that we lay out before us have many challenges, and our resolve to achieve the goals we have set is often the defining factor. From that, we make the decision between conformity and rebelliousness, or somewhere in between.

When one faces oppression or control-based rules when making a decision, they will also face life-altering choices that will surely weigh heavily upon them. Whether it takes great strength to accept and conform for the end result, or the greater strength is to assert one's free will, it carries with it no universal right or wrong. There is only the individual perception of what is the right thing for them to do, and that may include choosing against the standards or expectations of others.

As every card in a reading can represent a potential choice, this card reversed is certainly no different. We choose who, or what rules and traditions we follow and we decide why. This card reversed is essentially a presence of authority that is difficult, unjust, fraudulent, oppressive, or outright abusive. How you should choose to deal with it is not determined by this card's presence,

Lovers

UPRIGHT

Decisions involving love are often, if not always, the most emotionally charged choices we have to make. What lies at the heart of these decisions is commitment. A decision to make a commitment is often present here, but never a certainty. The certainty is a choice made through a cloud of emotion.

The strength of the euphoric feelings, which we first experience when love begins, will affect our decision-making, as will how we felt just prior to the inception of this new love. The decision to make a long-term commitment to someone is the most important decision we make, but the feelings that are associated with it can also alter one's judgment.

Imagine you have lived in the ruins of a recently past relationship that failed. You have swung back and forth between blaming the other person and yourself for not recognizing the signs of a bad relationship sooner. It's all behind you now and you have begun to move on with your life. Now you find yourself in the company of someone and your feelings start to grow. Will you be overly cautious or will you jump right in? This is the essence of the Lovers card. We are usually relegated to servitude of our hearts on matters of love, and we happily accept this as long as the feelings inside of us remain. However, the strength of these feelings are not all powerful, as they can be affected by our temptation to doubt. Therein the dilemma is found.

Which choice to make is not found in the cards, nor is it within these words. The decision is yours to make, and that is how it should be. This card calls to your attention the choice, and my intent is to help you understand why it has appeared.

There are no easy answers when it comes to decisions about love. Perhaps letting our heart, our inner most feelings guide us on such matters is by design. It certainly would seem that way since we are creatures with the ability to reason and doubt. Giving such powers to our feelings of love might actually be intended to push us beyond doubt and encourage us to reach out and fulfill our desire for close companionship.

REVERSED

A successful bond between two people requires a two-way flow of energy between the two. It is possible for one to give the illusion of reciprocating feelings, but it cannot be maintained over time. The illusion can often be bait and camouflage to prey on the vulnerable for personal gratification.

There are many aspects of this card to consider when it appears reversed, not the least of which is false love. Taking into account a current situation there may be jealousy or infidelity as the point of the question.

There are times we find ourselves in relationships with uncertainty about the other person, and we are left with only trust as our guide. However, consider which is more important; our trust in the other person, or our trust in our own judgment.

There is often a paradox found in the cards because they do not see absolutes, they see the outcome of the current path. That translates into the person with the question, if harboring unfounded suspicions, creating the conflict themselves in their own jealousy. One must take into account what they know, and find the true source of any suspicions they may have. Our life experiences shape our impressions of love and matters that carry strong emotions. It is difficult to ignore our past and it may make us more aware, or less trusting.

Evaluating a relationship just in itself is indicative of doubts and potential problems. A lot of the possibilities reflect only symptoms of bigger issues such as trust, loyalty, and intentions. Further examining these foundations of love within oneself is the best place to start before exploring them with one's partner. Open communication in a relationship is quite important, but probing and accusatory questions can create the self-fulfilling prophecy this card reversed has the potential to be describing in a reading.

Chariot

UPRIGHT

All of us have dreams of our future, and when these dreams become goals and ambitions then we begin to take action to realize them. This card defines those actions, and it can as well, help us mark progress along our path. The need to take action toward our goals and realize our dreams should emanate from the strength of our ambitions, but it isn't always that simple. When you ask questions about taking a new job or accepting an invitation, your dreams play a significant role in your decision.

Child prodigies aside, realizing dreams is a long and sometimes arduous journey. Understanding the impact of our decisions is not that difficult after they have been made and their effects have been determined. That can create situations of frustration and doubt if progress seems to be lost, even if there is a lesson of experience contained within.

When you contemplate a seemingly idle relationship or a career, you are looking for indications whether it is time to take action, or whether you should endure. We all have different degrees of tolerance, and passing those points often parallel a level of frustration. This of course can make for rash decisions.

The questions surrounding when to take action or when to endure may leave you looking for assurance that you are on the right track and can make this card a very helpful card when it appears.

The path will surely not be a straight line, with lateral movement, obstacles, and setbacks being common things to encounter and overcome as you move toward your goals. If you are sure and focused you will be able to achieve your goals and realize your dreams in time.

REVERSED

Taking action can be productive, or it can be counterproductive if it is done impulsively or out of frustration. When action is taken, it always affects others, and this must always be considered. A reckless disregard for the possible consequences to others when deciding to act extends well past the current circumstances, and even if it proves productive for one on a short-term basis, there is no guarantee it will be sustainable.

Personal gain and progress toward a goal are a significant part of the decision making process, but slipping into selfish, stubborn, and arrogant thinking is sometimes just one small step away. The line between making progress and proceeding at the expense of others can get blurry. How do you maintain a balance between assertively seeking to achieve your goals and the potentially damaging affects your actions may have on others. I can't imagine that a person of good conscience would normally have difficulty with this, but that is not to state that every inappropriate action is done with negligent disregard or malice.

It is also possible that not taking action when it is appropriate, necessary, and expected, could be revealed by the presence of this card in a reading.

Dreams become goals and ambitions, and our motivation propels us toward realizing them. How we navigate the path we have imagined before us will truly define us; much more so than the end result. That the end might justify the means doesn't protect even the most altruistic of ambitions when judgment is faced.

Intentions are only thoughts and words, and when the substance of appropriate action does not follow them, it will leave them merely empty promises. In the context of a reading, this card reversed depicts either needed action not taken, or a selfishly motivated push toward a personal goal. There are circumstances when the question that is asked will allow this card reversed to serve as a warning before action is taken.

Strength

UPRIGHT

The temptation to apply excessive force, whether it is physical or verbal, as the result of emotional stimulation or in defense of pride can be great, and strength is found in self-control.

Just because one can do something has absolutely no bearing on whether they should. Containing an emotional response, or to suffer one's pride, takes strength that cannot be quantified, but it is the essence of this card. Wisdom is a significant element that comes into play, but even the realization that control of one's action should be applied can be overwhelmed by strong emotions or damage to one's pride.

Our emotions are powerful forces that undeniably influence us, yet more importantly is how we turn them outward and use them to influence others and the situation at hand. When we feel something passionately, the need to express it can at times be hard to contain, and deciding how we will respond to others in such situations is a decision that is easily made when the waters are calm. However, the truth comes in the moment when the emotions are high. Therein lies the connection between wisdom and strength.

One must have the awareness to understand the need to choose wisely when circumstances confront us, but that is only the foundation of one's actions and reactions. When a moment arrives, the presence of mind must look to the foundation and one must have the strength to be true to the wisdom of that foundation.

Being caught up in the heat of the moment is a rationalization that comes after the occurrence. It is never a method of approach that is determined beforehand. The aforementioned post event description is a response to the realization that one's lack of strength has made things worse.

Strength prevails only in the moment; not in the foundation, nor in the aftermath. Some such moments may arise without warning while others may be clearly foreseen. A sudden impact upon one's emotions may illicit a quick and thoughtless reaction, and the anticipation of an emotionally charged event may allow for one's emotions to build momentum, but they both require strength of resolve to not make things worse; for others involved as well as oneself.

REVERSED

As I described in the upright interpretation of this card, emotions are powerful forces, and not only do they dominate our own actions, we turn them outward toward others as an intentional means of control over others. When this card is found reversed it goes beyond the weakness of the moment. It is brought about by a deep need to dominate and control others by using their emotions as a weapon against them. Manipulating others to overcome one's own weaknesses and further one's desire for gain is far from strength. There is no greater weapon to turn on someone than their own love, but by no means is this limited to strong feelings of love. It can apply to any person or situation where trust is involved.

From disheartening words expressed in anger toward the loving and trusting for the purpose of control, to being aggressive toward someone or something that threatens the ego or one's pride, when weakness attempts to portray itself as strength, you have one of the primary interpretations of this card. When weakness attempts to portray itself as strength you have one of the primary interpretations of this card.

There are other possibilities found in this card reversed and they all lead back to an inability or unwillingness to practice self-control. The definitive element is weakness; whether the behavior exhibited is malevolent, compensation, or wounded pride, it should be easily recognizable within the context of the situation.

It may serve as a warning where temptation is high and great inner strength is required, or an indicator of what might be approaching from an external source. In many cases it could be unavoidable when it represents the actions of others and its appearance should prepare you. The ability to avoid it might require the bending of one's own free will, and in some instances, there may not be any way to avoid it when it is a behavioral trait in another person that one cares about.

Hermit

UPRIGHT

There is a need within us to evaluate ourselves, understand ourselves, and seek greater enlightenment, and as is often the case in the Tarot cards, there is a metaphorical representation depicted in this one as well. Creating great physical distance between people, situations, and distractions, is not the truth within this card.

If the physical distance represented in this card becomes the primary focus, it is likely to become the justification for avoiding introspection and enlightenment. To seek enlightenment from a higher power or to achieve a better understanding of one's own feelings through introspection does not require distance – only time set aside to be only with oneself. How far we physically travel is inconsequential to what we can accomplish. Improving ourselves and the situations around us requires only that we actually seek to do so.

The blocking out of external influences and distractions has become more difficult than our ancestors could ever have imagined. Finding time, or actually taking it, has become something that can easily be dismissed as our desires to interact with others, born of our nature as social creatures, can instantly be fulfilled everywhere we travel.

We no longer find ourselves with natural periods of time that provide us with opportunity to explore ourselves with introspection; we must with specific purpose deliberately create it and resist the ease of constant access to others. Taking time to reflect upon ourselves in sensory isolation now requires an effort to do so, as it is seldom ever provided as an opportunity to take.

The choices we make along the paths that we take are our own, and external influences must be considered for their value to us and our goals. That is seldom done when the influences are so easily accessible and persistent. That one just doesn't have the time is only a matter of an unwillingness to make it available.

REVERSED

There are times in our lives when events can cause us to seek solitude and hide within ourselves. Such things as bereavement and illness are possible reasons for isolation, but there are many more to consider. Fear may as well be at the heart of one's withdraw.

When mourning a loss there is sometimes a desire to be alone, and of course everyone deals with these events differently. This possibility may be the hardest to come back from, but at some point in time one must still face the world, and if necessary begin anew. This card reversed describes a need to evaluate the situation, and understand what is influencing one's choices.

The desire or decision to withdraw may begin with temporary intentions and become overwhelmingly comfortable over time. The difference is significant between isolating oneself for introspection, and hiding from the world in fear, the result of feelings generated by low self-esteem.

The cycle of self-isolation may fuel the reclusiveness as one becomes hypersensitive around others and feelings of social ineptitude permeate their thoughts. However, getting used to being alone, even claiming to be perfectly happy with it, is actually denial. A person can live comfortably alone without perceived expectations and demands, but we aren't really meant to live that way. Inside us all is emptiness when in solitude no matter how much we rationalize or deny it; we are not creatures of isolation.

Temporary moments of isolation for contemplation, grief, recovery, and to seek enlightenment, are important, but progress upon one's path is at a standstill when one does not make an effort to get back into the flow. The paths that we each follow as individuals do not find us; we must actively find and follow them.

If one has concluded that their destiny has been realized and they have reached the pinnacle of their possibilities when they are alone, isolating themselves from others, they are only rationalizing their fear of continuing.

Wheel of Fortune

UPRIGHT

Good fortune is a stickler for gratitude and acknowledgment, but is repulsed by dependence. The act of searching for luck amounts to being prepared and aware when an opportunity presents itself, and from that point being humble in the blessing bestowed upon one.

Although good fortune is not something that one can count on, it may serve to enhance one's life if one is not dependent upon it or is not expecting it to rescue them from troubled times. There are times when it will appear when you need it the most, but it doesn't relate to the need; it comes because you are aware of the possibilities and your hope rings positive. Powerful positive thoughts, optimism, and prayer work, but not necessarily as an external force that changes your life for you. Any person who practices these behaviors possesses a strong belief in something: a change for the better. Their expectations influence awareness, and in turn they are prepared for opportunity.

We are extremely predisposed to seeing what we expect to see, and that statement is the truth behind good fortune. By no means am I discounting or even attempting to diminish a greater force found in the beliefs of many, as what I describe here is the one thing every belief has in common when it comes to good fortune.

If one wishes to acknowledge a celestial entity of any variation as the provider of fortuitous events then by all means do so, but consider the power of free will upon the situation. The events that make up our lives are the results of our decisions, and if we are influenced by heavenly or psychic forces, that is all they really are, influences. How one generates the strength to believe that good things will happen may be relevant in building the foundation for one's attitude, but it doesn't make the choice, the one does.

REVERSED

On the inverse side of good luck is of course bad luck. What is it about misfortune that seems to put down roots in one's life and make them feel as if it will never end? If you follow the same line of thinking involving expectations you have one answer. An aspect that may make it more difficult is that negative thoughts seem to come easier to some, and they may tend to embrace them as a rationale for their choices.

In the larger picture, this card reversed can mean just that, bad choices. If you look at it closely it is not hard to see why the decision making process is likely to perpetuate the situation when one finds themselves living in the wake of a perceived unlucky event. As I mentioned, there is a direct correlation between what one expects to happen and how their awareness leads one right to it.

Looking closely at the events that make up our lives, they generally go our way or they don't. That makes our point of view the most significant element when it comes to our fortunes. Now having said that, when it comes to luck, specifically misfortune, deferring responsibility to bad luck is another way to absolve oneself of blame and responsibility, and that is a strong possibility here.

There are many things that happen out of our control, and although we may sometimes affect them, there are times we can only accept them. However, when you look at the trail of decisions that lead to events there could very well be a clear path one has created. That leads to the ever handy scapegoat of bad luck. Consider that our perceptions lead us to choices, and those choices in turn lead to events. We then evaluate the results of these events based on our perceptions.

What will befall one when this card appears reversed is going to be perceived as misfortune, but it is not a harbinger of perpetual bad luck. It will only manifest as something that will seem not to go in one's favor. How it affects one is relative and may appear small or large in one's eyes, and that is the point of perspective.

It is important to weigh expectations when one has a turn of bad luck, as they will certainly have an effect on what one is aware of, and easily influence choices. There is a certainty of life that things will not go in one's favor from time to time, and the matter at hand is how that affects a person's attitude and outlook.

Justice

UPRIGHT

To be fair, is where this card begins and ends. Any legal system exists to right a wrong, and there is no openly expressed contention to the contrary. Whether it be Karmic justice or a legal determination, it is a certainty that achieving balance is what is represented here. The likelihood that this is a turn for the better is relative to where it falls in a reading and the circumstances of the current situation. Then there is one's expectations and perceptions to consider as well.

We all are inflicted with subjectivity to varying degrees, and the balance of fairness one expects will not always be contained within the confines of a single situation or circumstance. Beyond any doubt that is the most significant element to understand.

Our legal systems are designed to provide a level of justice, obviously, but their primary purpose is to maintain order by attempting to take emotion and subjectivity out of the equation. From the human perspective this limits fairness to the elements surrounding a singular event, and at times they can provide a successful remedy. However, it is inescapable that human justice exists on the micro level and true fairness for all must be determined on a much broader scale as might be defined as a macro justice, or in a word, Karma.

Justice is not designed to be revenge or getting back at someone, it is equilibrium in the simplest sense. If one uses the phrase, *what you deserve*, it should unequivocally be a positive sentiment, not born of emotions and vengeance.

The likeliest reasons for this card to appear upright are legal determinations or a restoring of balance, and they are not always synonymous. When one feels wronged, the emotional strength it takes to endure and allow Karma to run its course is substantial, and I am not attempting to make any decisions for them in these words. However, there is an infinite cycle that one can become trapped in when one chooses to put their thumb on the scale and establish their perceived idea of fairness.

REVERSED

The reverse interpretation of this card often has little to do with legal adjudication or the balancing of Karma, although it cannot be completely excluded in some situations. What is applicable here are the human elements of predisposition, judgment, malice, or revenge, and try as you might with clear heart you cannot fit fair into the same sentence with any of these concepts. From that, it should be easy to realize that when one is presiding over decisions that affect others, one's own interest or beliefs take precedence, and are the decision making factor in the described situation.

Feelings of being wronged can be powerful motivators to take unjust action, and can be easily rationalized in one's own mind as being only fair. Whether are not the other person's actions were intentional, the far-reaching ripple effects of all those involved are discarded if one has reached this state of thinking. Even beyond that lies bias and prejudice, and an "every person for themselves" mentality. There is a certainty that others will be unfairly treated in any one of these cases, and furthermore, how one feels about others or their actions is a matter of judgment, not justice. When one succumbs to the temptation of deciding another person or their actions are inappropriate or less worthy than their own, then the true crux of this card reversed is realized.

On the terrestrial level we appoint, elect, and recruit others like us to make determinations of judgment upon those who have acted against the best interest of others. These are quite elaborate systems and we simplify it with the words "fair trial," and we take some level of comfort in the court's practices because of those two simple words.

We place a lot of reverence on the word fair, as we should, but as I mentioned earlier, the primary significance of a terrestrial legal system is order, and its ability to be successful rests on taking absolute power away from those who feel as if they have been wronged. To be emotionally charged, biased, prejudiced, or inappropriately aggressive, can form the basis of action that will in fact place one on the receiving end of justice, when all is said and done. Our ability to care about others is inherent, and should be applied, just as we care about ourselves.

When this card appears reversed it may be because Karma has come calling, and Universal justice is being served. Or it may be that someone has led themselves to believe that they too carry their own sword of justice, and are pursuing their personal perception of fair.

Hanged Man

UPRIGHT

The interpretation of this card often points to a decision one must make between what they *want* to do, and what they *should* do, or in other words, when the right thing to do is different from the desire. I prefer not to use the word sacrifice for the upright description, although it is commonly used, and in some situations might be accurate. My reasoning is that by definition it strips one of any benefit by making the decision to go against what they would rather choose. There are many occasions where the needs of others, and oneself, are met by choosing against what one wants. With children to feed and bills to pay, going to work for many isn't their first choice, but it is the right choice. This card can represent something that basic when it appears, or it could mean much more as well.

Independence has a number of limiting aspects that deprive it of its purity, and there is certain to be a level of dependency in any relationship. Consider that offering emotional support for someone should not be thought of as a sacrifice, and is a staple of many types of relationships. There are people who put others first without hesitation or reservation, no matter the situation, and there are those who might need a little convincing. It isn't that the latter described is any less a good person, as we are designed to look out for our own best interest, it is the nature of survival. It is by way of comparison that it would appear that way.

This card can be interpreted as a message for someone who has been acting unselfishly to take some time for his or her personal interest, or as an influence for one to recognize a need in another. This really emphasizes a change in one's thinking, perhaps not dramatically, but at least a reevaluation of the balance of attention given to oneself and others.

There are more demanding possibilities here, for example, providing care for an ill relative, which equates to putting one's own dreams on hold. Overall, this card expresses, as many cards do, a need to look closely at the current situation and determine what matters to the people one cares about, and in truth, what kind of person they would need to be to make the right decision.

REVERSED

It may have begun with a willingness to give of oneself, and maybe it did not, but in either case, resentment toward another is still a possibility here. Often represented in this card reversed is regret over previous choices, and this could lead to demands of obligation where one is now brandishing their perceived sacrifice as a debt that must be repaid.

It certainly is not unheard of for someone to list their perceived sacrifices, for the purpose of manipulating a situation for their own benefit. When two people really do care about each other, there will be no mention of sacrifice, and the very word will not be heard in any conversations regarding their actions toward each other. When this card appears reversed, one has come to believe that the situation is unfair, and that belief might be real or perceived. An obvious element here would be selfishness, either in unwillingness to give, or demanding a sacrifice from another.

Beyond the one-on-one relationship aspect is the possibility of resistance to choices in the interest of the greater good where several others are involved. There are people who would thrive on this sense of power, and since they feel they're holding all the cards it should be worth something. Doing the right thing for the right price would qualify as extortion in no uncertain terms.

Any situation where one is feeling forced, or even compelled, to make a decision against what they know is right would constitute a sacrifice. The interpretation of this card when found reversed describes any decision or action that is unduly forced upon another, or withheld by someone in selfishness.

One could also view this as one sacrificing another to serve their own interest, even if it is just for the sake of controlling them. The desire to control someone, or a situation, lies at the depths of the interpretation here. There might be a direct approach or passive-aggressive manipulation, but one's goal is using or doing the right thing only for self-interest.

Death

UPRIGHT

There is no direct connection to actual death regarding the physical body of the querent or others they might know in the interpretation of this card. That is extremely important to consider since taking the meaning of this card by its title is actually missing the point entirely. A certainty in life is that things never stay the same, and this card represents sometimes traumatic and often unexpected change.

Due to its traditional label, and in no small part the result of theatrical depiction, this is the most frequently misunderstood card in a Tarot deck. The word death is ominous, much more so than the word change, and when something alters one's life so dramatically that it seems to shatter their dreams of the future, it deserves to have the stronger description. Each situation will be viewed in relative terms by those involved, and what it represents to them will have the weight they themselves give the event.

Someone will experience an event that will make their future different than they expected. The end of a relationship, the loss of a job, and moving to a different location, are realistic examples of change. There are numerous possibilities that could apply, including an event that shakes the foundation of what one believes.

How things are now and how they will be in the future will be altered by a single point in time when someone or something will affect a change. The vitally significant thing to remember is that this event will by perception portray a foreboding view of the aftereffects of the change. However, that does not have to be the case unless one cannot let go of what was, and embrace what now is, or will be.

It might possibly be difficult, and as relative as that is to the one going through it, the ability to overcome it is certain. Whether one accepts the change or does not is the only choice this card depicts. This is not a change that will destroy the path, as one's path will always lie before them, but there is likely to be a need for adjustments, and as well, such an event should influence a reevaluation and may result in a new direction for the path.

REVERSED
In the aftermath of dramatic change is a need to accept and continue on, and the truth of the matter is one simply has no choice. This card reversed points to a situation, where at the very least, one is struggling with what is different after a change. Stagnation and debilitating emotions such as self-pity following a change that one is unwilling to accept are very common here. One might feel lonely, depressed, or slip into fear about future possibilities, and it can all be traced to an inability to let go of the past and move on. Finding oneself in a different situation than was once envisioned as one's future can be daunting, but not impossible to overcome. One's resolve is what must be examined.

A person's expectations do not always match how events unfold and here is a needed adjustment to a difference that one is not accepting. The longer that negative feelings are allowed to live in one's thoughts the worse the situation or circumstances will become. A spiraling affect that will continue until it is faced, addressed, and overcome with resolve and determination.

Aside from marrying people that we are in love with, we also grow attached to our futures, falling in love and marrying them as well. It is easy to see how this compounds the difficulty when relationships end or circumstances do not match the envisioned future. In this situation, one's path has changed and perhaps years and years have been invested toward what was once the expected future.

We are paradoxical creatures who find extreme comfort in familiarity, while at the same time we survive due to our inherent ability to adapt to change. This is an internal struggle between emotions and instincts, where how bad one feels pins them to ground, and one can't seem to find the strength to get back up.

I should not have to express here that one cannot survive, let alone thrive if they are not even trying to adapt. The interpretation of this card reversed represents what one *will not* do, not what one *cannot* do. How easy it is, isn't for me to decide, nor does this card reversed express the difficulty either, only that it needs to be done.

Temperance

UPRIGHT

Being forced to choose between the drive for a sense of greater achievement, and those who cherish one's presence in their lives can be quite difficult at times. We have to do what we have to do, that much is certain, but what of the situations where the pursuit of one's personal goals have completely taken over their list of priorities? Of course, such pursuits are important and they do belong on the list, however, what of the people who have invited one into their lives to share other things?

    The appearance of this card is an indication that one should look more closely at the situation and address it appropriately, not entirely for the sake of others, but for oneself as well. The words responsibility and obligation are applied to what takes one away from people and situations, and that moves in both directions. Which direction, is defined by when one feels like they would rather be elsewhere doing something else entirely.

One may need to go to work, and may desire to do so to fulfill part of their dream, yet what brings them home should not be a feeling of obligation, but a desire to be there when they can. That is what balance represents, and again what is being described here does not always mean equal parts; instead, it describes the decisions that are made when one truly does have a choice.

There are numerous career paths that require a lot of time and effort in order to excel, and that should be understood by all those involved. On the other hand, if one presumes that who is at home waiting will always be there when one decides to visit them, they may one day discover their presumption was false.

There should be adjustments, understanding, and even compromise, but anything else may be taking someone for granted. The interpretation of this card will allow for the inverse of what I have described, and may depict a priority list that is in complete disarray. Somewhere, and for some currently unknown reason, perhaps even masked by denial, an important aspect of one's life is not receiving adequate attention.

REVERSED

Upright interpretations can serve as notices or warnings with the purpose of prompting awareness in situations, whereas what is represented by the reverse of the card can describe extremes and/or that a threshold has been crossed. Beyond unchecked imbalance one will find stress and desperate acts. The expression burnout can certainly be considered here as things have gotten so far out of hand one is having a difficult time coping, let alone adjusting and seeking to regain balance.

A feeling of critical mass may exist within one as they feel nothing they do will resolve the situation, and their actions may be born of irrational thinking. When one believes they have lost control of the situation, with any semblance of control probably having been a false assumption in the first place, they can find themselves in crisis mode leading to high drama and desperation. Minor conflicts can become catastrophic as one seeks to turn back time and regain control.

When this card appears reversed there are likely warnings that have been missed or ignored and a line has now been crossed. One cannot fight to recover from this situation; they must accept and learn, and evaluate their thoughts and actions, finding their way forward again. When one proceeds under circumstances that are not in balance, they will eventually reach a point of disregard and neglect, and this is not something others will tolerate for very long.

The most important element to consider here is that if one has not yet lost someone or something, it may not be very far away. If one is stubbornly retaining an improper mindset and attitude, there will eventually be an impact with reality, and it will not go well at all. A singular focus of one's energy in a different direction will not go unnoticed by others, and one should not only take the time, they should make the time count.

Even if one does care for the feelings of others, it is not going to look that way if only promising words are offered as a resolution. If one now finds oneself suffering a loss, then the time to make a change may have passed.

Devil

UPRIGHT

Here we have an indulgence that at the very least is a hindrance; an obstacle to one's progress that one carries around with them wherever they go. This may represent an addiction, an affliction, obsession, or self-absorbed hedonism. From a simple distraction, all the way up to a self-described, rationalized need that threatens one's mortality. It may involve one's need to escape a personal perception of themselves or their environment, and thus a cycle exists that one can feel trapped in, blaming others, and stagnating. The difficulty with this card most often lies in denial because if one sees their behavior for what it really is, they are more likely to make different choices. Yes, of course, easier said than done, but that is rationalization as well.

Where and when does *need to change* meet *want to change*? Therein lies the key to different choices. Would a Tarot card or such words written in a book have the power to change the thinking, where friends and loved ones may have already failed? One has to see a self-inflicted obstacle for what it is before there can be any hope at all, and that is an internal process.

Loved ones have the ability to influence a possible choice, but in the face of a threat to alter the situation, perhaps the ending of a relationship, then one's motivation may be to avoid a situation they do not want to live through. In something of a tragic irony, avoiding things they do not want to experience is what they do already with escapism, so false promises would come naturally. In no way, shape, fashion, or form, am I encouraging someone to suffer within the destructive patterns of another; I am merely pointing out that if one wants to be around such a person, contingent on a change in their behavior, realize what you may be up against.

To reiterate my position, these words are not advice, but observations concerning the interpretations of this card. When it appears in a reading there is an unbalanced, if not destructive, force affecting the situation, and how one chooses to approach it and deal with it can only truly come from inside that person. That much is simple.

REVERSED

That one is now focused upon the changes that are needed to overcome the behaviors that are holding them back, might be a good interpretation to start with when this card is found reversed. This is often considered to be a matter of meeting the challenges with strength from within as the first step back towards progress. Other entities, terrestrial or celestial, may play a role but the power to proceed appropriately always begins within.

The perspective of having freed oneself, as a sense of completion, is a bit tricky because some addictions and behaviors might only be temporarily subdued, and must be resisted for an indeterminate amount of time. The interpretation of this card begins and ends with the will to move beyond the problem and continue to leave it behind.

This card can describe a situation where one is seeking out help through family, friends, or professionals, but the underlying element of this card reversed still remains if they are in truth willing to try to overcome what holds them back. In fairness, circumstances might be compelling one to seek help, and questions about their commitment may linger, but it is an opportunity that represents a first step.

Aside from risky, harmful and extremely dangerous activities there are other behavioral distractions that negate progress and one should not narrowly construe the possibilities by limiting it to only drugs and alcohol for instance. There are many types of habitual or pattern behaviors one might posses that can create difficulty for themselves and others, even if it seems harmless.

One should give others the benefit of the doubt if they appear to meet the criteria of what this card represents. Challenging one's sincerity and resolve may motivate them, but it can also work against progress if they do not feel supported in their efforts.

Some cards speak in terms of encouragement more than enlightenment, and that may be the case here. Some things simply take time and attempting to overcome bad habits in a single stroke is somewhat unrealistic. Overconfidence may lead one to unnecessarily challenge their strength and resolve, before they are actually as strong as they see themselves.

Tower

UPRIGHT

Is this bad? Yes, but how bad is better left to one's perspective. This card represents a situation where one is now standing amid the rubble of something they once believed in, possibly unsure of what went wrong. It is easy me for me to say without any stake in the situation, but the most important element here is what one discovers and learns from what has happened. Whatever one has lost or destroyed, it is only a portion of how bad it could have been, or someday will be, if one does not get the message.

A likely possibility here is hubris, where one had come to believe they could not fail and completely disregarded any warning signs. When one's confidence is mixed with success, reward, and recognition, at times it can take on a life of its own. One might also consider inexperience with the workings of the endeavor they took on and felt compelled to proceed to prove the doubters wrong. Whether proceeding with arrogance or protecting one's pride, it is highly likely this situation was avoidable. Some things are certainly out of one's control, but there are always choices along the way that, when improperly made, can cause one to relinquish control.

Another element along those lines is seeing the potential for collapse and deflecting responsibility to others instead of seeking to rectify the situation. Even beyond that is sabotage where the intention was never to succeed but to undermine someone else with false information. One should notice the constant here is that the catastrophic event will not be a surprise to everyone.

Whether it is due to arrogant thinking, ignorance, denial, or maliciousness, this situation is the result of someone's mindset and purpose. Remembering that the cards only describe possibilities, not absolutes, adjustments could possibly be made that would avert disaster, but one has to accept the reality of the circumstances first.

The interpretation of this card is more about what went wrong than the actual event, and future outcomes will be affected by how one responds to this situation. That sentiment may not be very comforting to some, and depending on the nature of the event, it may take time to recover and see through the feelings of loss, but an honest evaluation is necessary.

REVERSED

There are two very significant possibilities in this card reversed, and they both reflect an acceptance and understanding of what did or is about to go wrong. This amounts to a lesson learned in the wake of disaster or just in time to keep one from happening. To begin with, this describes an improvement in one's perspective, not just regarding the current situation, but also in all things going forward, an enlightenment that brings with it a positive outlook. The catastrophic event is the point of impact upon one's mindset, either in the awakening of one's foresight or an epiphany in hindsight. The primary representation of this card reversed is best described as an evolution of one's thinking, and disaster, or near disaster, should get one's attention.

The elements that should stand out are humility, gratitude, and expressions of regret toward others who were affected by one's previous choices. All of one's actions affect others and sometimes quite dramatically; setting things right is a step toward growth and enlightenment.

The change here is primarily internal, and although there may be differences in the environment, the primary focus remains on the one who has something to learn. This is not to diminish any tragedy by any means, its purpose is making things better for one in the future.

I am intentionally not putting any emphasis on the event, since one does not need me, or a Tarot card to tell them when something is bad. What this offers might be described as redemption, or another chance at something important, and a significant transition in one's attitude and perspective can require a significant event to be realized.

There may be an element of putting things back together again, mending fences and trying to rebuild burnt bridges. Even if it is hard, fixing the past does not mean dwelling on it; the future is where one needs to look in the aftermath. Feelings of shame or humiliation are possible, but they are extremely counterproductive and should be discarded. The difficulty of the situation is of course relative and I am not saying get over it, but instead get through it, and it will get better.

Star

UPRIGHT

Amidst struggles and difficult times, one may look to the heavens for a glimmer of hope that there will be better times ahead, and this card is the response one wants to find. When one is trapped in the bleakness of things not going one's way, seemingly with no end in sight, the interpretation of this card speaks of an impending change in the situation.

This might be considered a card of encouragement that renews confidence and strength to endure for just a little longer in the aftermath of recent events that may have brought about difficult times and emotional suffering. Feeling hope is an emotional difference maker in the face of opportunity, and the key to this card is in believing that things will get better.

There is truth to the sentiment that one will find the future one expects to find. Is it manifestation, or a keener awareness of opportunities and the confidence to act upon them? It is your choice actually, as the mind will create a path to the future you envision, whether it is good or bad. How you perceive it to be realized, as in why you are optimistic, is not an element that should be evaluated. It is only important that you have faith in whatever you believe will make the difference, and in what should not be a revelation, that would be you.

When situations are less than desirable, or even tragic, the single aspect that one can control with certainty is how they handle it and move toward their future. I am certainly not proclaiming it to be easy; sometimes a ray of hope, a star in the heavens, is needed to bolster confidence and that is the primary meaning, or purpose, of this card when it appears in a reading.

The significant elements that apply to this card are rooted in one's outlook and positive expectations. There may be moments of inspiration where one finds new solutions to problems and insight into overcoming obstacles that previously seemed overwhelming. Such inspirations and new ideas may have an external source, but one must be in the right mindset to recognize them. The renewed strength to set aside worry, doubt, and fears, to face challenges with decisiveness and purpose are the takeaway in this card, however the resolve is acquired.

REVERSED

Many of us are familiar with the curse that seems to apply to the words, *things can't get any worse*. It's as if a challenge has been thrown down to prove one wrong and the Universe or some celestial entity is happy to oblige. The statement sounds innocuous enough, but it is usually uttered in resignation over a situation that is perceived to be as bad as it can get, obviously.

The interpretation of this card is based on elements such as despair, hopelessness, and resignation. One feels as if they are falling farther than they could hope to survive. They have lost all faith in themselves and frequently entertain thoughts of being undeserving, inadequate, and unable to recover. There is no floor to interpreting this card when it appears reversed; it can reach all the way down to depression and tragic thoughts.

I am not diminishing anyone's state of difficulty or crisis by stating that all things are relative to the individual and things are seldom as bad as they seem. All things rightfully live in the perspective of the individual, but that is the actual point here. Each of us has a primal system built in that initiates actions that are meant to ensure our survival, but as powerful as this inherent first priority is, it can be completely shut down by one's emotional state of mind.

Resignation is acceptance, perhaps by deflecting responsibility to fate or in some fashion relinquishing control of outcomes to others and punctuating it with, *what's the point?* When one finds this card reversed in a reading, in a position that relates directly to them, will they say, "That's me," or will they say, "That is wrong; it will get better"?

There isn't any weakness in doubt. We all have it at times and it can be prudent, but it is not a strength either. Doubt should help influence good decision making, not become a debilitating fear that makes all the decisions on its own. The significant difference between the interpretation of this card upright and what it means reversed can be as simple as not seeing hope and most likely because one is not looking.

The elements described can as well be viewed as symptoms of one's mental state, brought out to be realized. If the situation is bad a Tarot card is not going to appear for the purpose of confirming what one already feels, that would actually further the despair. This is a card that should be disagreed with and proven wrong.

Moon

UPRIGHT

This is a very unusual card in its interpretation because it suggests that something is not known, which of course stands to reason if one has just asked a question for the purpose of a reading. Looking beyond that we are apt to find confusion, possibly apprehension. There has to be a reason for one's uncertainty, but when left undiscovered and unexamined that can lead to doubt and even fear. Things we do not know or understand become sounds in the shadows that seem likely to catch us off guard, and yet we are keenly aware that a mystery surrounds the situation.

Now the question becomes, whether we should be afraid of something just because we don't know what it is or anything about how we know it is there. If one thinks through the situation they will likely discover that the answer is found in the decisions they made to get to this point. The choices we make are how we navigate our path and when circumstances do not seem clear to us it is often due to searching externally for the answers that are actually found within.

That leads us to psychic awareness and things we sense, feel, or even know, when we really do not know why we know them. Is one afraid of something because one does not know what it is, or because one does know and doesn't understand how one knows. One must accept and embrace one's psychic awareness, and utilize it to make the correct choices. That is the basis of this card.

There is also the possibility of illusions or deceptions in the situation when this card appears in a reading. However, by evaluating the steps that led you to this point and trusting your feelings, then determining the appropriateness of fear is accurately realized.

Experiencing moments of concern and fear are defense mechanisms designed to protect us, and the ability to see fears as rational or unfounded is built into us as well. Finding this card in a reading suggests a time to explore your feelings to find the answer to your confusion and apprehension.

REVERSED

In simplified terms, this card reversed is clarity. This is the understanding of a situation and the circumstances that surround one, leading to decisiveness about whether to proceed or withdraw. When faced with the unknown, decisions can become great obstacles, and here the path is clear. Your thinking should now lead to action and progress or at the very least the avoidance of a setback.

We process more information than we are consciously aware of and the presumption that we are constantly in touch with everything that touches us is inaccurate. You can test this by thinking about what you are doing right now. You are obviously reading a book, and your conscious mind is likely devoted to the words on the page. Now allow yourself to become aware of what else is going on around you right now. Other elements of your environment are still being processed by the brain, but considered secondary and set aside; for example such things as background noises unless they become obtrusive, or are a trigger, such as your name being spoken, that activates a conscious awareness.

There are similarities between this card and the High Priestess, but once you explore them further you can see the difference. They both promote psychic awareness, with the High Priestess describing an available higher state of consciousness, a seemingly hidden source of knowledge. Whereas this card, both upright and reversed, tells of a need to apply it to your current situation.

Another possible aspect of this card reversed is that it is capable of portraying the exposure of deceit, fraud, or denial in a situation. This includes self-denial and deceit perpetrated upon oneself. In the end it comes down to awareness in all instances, and not being resistant to thoughts or feelings on the basis that the source of the information cannot be trusted because it is indefinable.

Sun

UPRIGHT

This is a positive card and the situation will improve when this card appears in a reading. There are no defined absolutes here and it will apply to the individual in a relative way.

    This is frequently interpreted as a vast improvement, perhaps in hopefulness, but it is no less true that one will feel good about the situation in the future. One should greatly consider the role of outlook when this card appears. Expectations will rise as blessings are received and appreciated, and the ability to look forward with confidence will influence how positive one now feels. The positive events that will happen can be such things as agreements reached and partnerships formed in pursuit of an even greater goal, with everything pointing toward progress and achievement.

    What victories and accomplishments that are achieved here can be substantial and worth celebrating, but that is not the overall representation. The results will bring greater and more enthusiastic focus upon the possibilities of realizing more distant goals, while at the same time reminding one to savor the journey. Looking forward to a day when a dream will be realized can on occasion blind one to the blessings they could enjoy now.

Physical life is too short to put all things positive off—waiting for events to transpire that will provide happiness and fulfillment. Without enjoying the journey what will one come to feel in the anticipated moments when they do arrive?

This is not intended to discourage diligence, resulting in the abandonment of the necessary commitment to proceed successfully on the path toward the dream, but to encourage one to be aware in the present and experience it fully as well. The sentiment, "I will be happy when," would be better expressed, "I will be happier when." This is the significant aspect of this card to consider when it is found in a reading.

REVERSED

Obviously pessimism and doubt about the future will steal away one's ability to be happy in the present, but so too will relentlessly pushing oneself without regard for the current situation. As the upright interpretation refers to the positives one should be aware of, the reverse of this card points out that one has slipped deeper into allowing only possible future events to dictate how one feels now.

The most important element to consider here is the feeling of powerlessness, as in the inability to control how future events transpire. To be complacent and accepting in circumstances is relinquishing one's ability to affect change with choice, and making all things externally realized. *Going with the flow* does not mean giving in. Instead, it describes *change what you can and accept what you cannot.*

The interpretation of this card, upright and reversed, is outlook based, and does not mean that bad things will happen when it appears this way; it means that one expects them to happen. It is possible that recent disappointments are fostering a negative outlook, altering expectations, but the future is only negatively impacted by past events if one allows it to happen.

There is the possibility that there are others involved in the situation that are promoting negative thinking with disparaging comments and a negative outlook of their own. The source of such influences may have their own agenda and will benefit from one's failure, destroying confidence with remarks of doom and gloom that are intended to undermine one's ability to succeed.

A constant and overwhelming feeling of optimism is the part that is truly unrealistic, but one's outlook will most certainly affect decisiveness and the quality of the choices one makes. Furthermore, dashed hopes can wear one down, making each decision harder than the last one, so there is no perfect here, only the need for effort in attitude as well as the endeavor. One could choose to view this card reversed as depicting a crossroads in their thinking and attitude, where one either worries the present away, or counts their blessings.

Judgment

UPRIGHT

Judgment is an inescapable part of life for each and every one of us. It is as certain as one's next breath, and the only absolute connection it has to what a person believes is what others think about that chosen belief. Will we each one day be judged by an agent of a celestial overseer? Don't know, haven't been there, haven't done that, yet. However, there are those that proclaim this to be a certainty, and they judge those who do not agree with them. In turn, the judged then judge the judges as being judgmental. Sorry about that last sentence, but the point is that judgment is a perpetuating cycle of decisions based on agree or disagree, like or dislike, do this or do that, and on and on. In all likelihood you are forming a judgment right now about me and what I am expressing.

Most of us want to be viewed favorably in all areas of our lives: how we make ourselves look, how we dress, our thoughts and opinions, and of course our decision making, which governs almost everything about us. Since our decisions reflect our judgment, we want to be judged as having good judgment. Before I get too far down that road again, simply put, a decision is a judgment, and we make them every day, often without conscious awareness.

The heart of this card is a positive assessment of one's choices and most likely administered on a terrestrial level. Since there is so much judgment going on around us all the time, the possibilities are practically endless. One should consider more significant aspects of their life as the cards are not often trivial, and what this card refers to will have an impact on one's path. It may be a beneficial legal adjudication in one's favor, or a career advancement that pushes one forward along their path.

There may be a connection to love and romance where another reveals their interest has increased after experiences together have offered insight into what truly lies in one's heart. A positive evaluation begins and ends with a person doing the right thing and not acting in their own best interest. This card may also reveal that one is of a mind to pass good judgment upon another.

REVERSED

To be thought of in a negative light, perhaps unfairly, is what one should consider here. A negative judgment placed on one often results in a setback to the thought process, and it is further magnified if the assessment is perceived to be unfair. It doesn't matter how hard one tries to do the right thing, and make the right decisions; there will always be detractors, with a negative or critical view. How one allows this to affect their own self-evaluation, planning, and progress upon their path is important.

Determining the value of the judgment or criticism is separating the good from the bad and requires one to be honest with themselves. Whether it is accurate or unfair, they both offer an opportunity to progress even if it results in a temporary setback. If it is valid criticism, then being stubborn and unyielding will not be productive, and if one deems it to be inaccurate and fixates on being unfairly judged, this will also negate progress.

To feel as if every decision can be made correctly and that one will never suffer from unfair criticism is unrealistic. There will always be a need for acceptance in regards to the judgments of others, whether they are truly meant to help or if they are intended to hurt.

Obstacles, as reversed cards often represent, may arise from the actions of others but they can also be self-inflicted barriers. Determining the intent of a negative assessment is for one to decide in their own evaluation of the circumstances. In understanding the situation one can then choose how best to proceed.

In the context of the situation one should also consider what may be at the heart of what judgments they are passing on others. Are any criticisms that are being expressed truly constructive or serving one's own needs or desires? Moreover, such judgments do not have to be verbally expressed to alter the situation, as any negative reaction will affect one's perception of others and the situation.

One's personal assessments can be influenced by envy or fear, and with very little effort, a word or two spoken to others can gain momentum and the one judging will find themselves being judged. Of course there are always going to be situations where one believes they have made an accurate assessment and it may seem beneficial to make others aware; however, everyone has their own perspectives, and not all will agree.

World

UPRIGHT

This card has the ability to be either simple or complex in its interpretation. It can represent the accomplishment of a singular goal, or it can describe where many different elements of one's life come together and fulfillment is realized. The long and often arduous path to achievement is soon to be rewarded and one's desire for success in their endeavor will be true.

We are by nature goal-oriented creatures and this is infinitely perpetual over the course of our lifetimes. When one has something to look forward to, there is purpose to their life, and although multiple objectives may overlap, the completion of one should be followed by the defining of another. There is often found to be happiness in the quest itself with the conclusion only representing one step before the next beginning.

The dream of a loving and fulfilling relationship, family and friends, and a successful career, is pretty much a part of all our lives at sometime. When it comes to fruition, we can feel as if we are on top of the world, and by no coincidence, that can very well be the interpretation of this card.

One's expectations and perceptions are always relative and if one is always looking for the greener grass then the likelihood of ever experiencing the feelings that this card is describing are not very good. Certain aspects of the dream can be improved upon while happiness and fulfillment remain intact, such as a nicer house or a job promotion. If one views other elements with the need for improvement, it may be reflective of perpetual dissatisfaction and that requires an evaluation of oneself before questioning the situation.

This is not to say people and situations cannot change, altering the perspective, but shallowness and materialistic values are not going to be a part of true happiness and fulfillment. In that mindset there will always be better-looking people, or better lovers; better jobs or bigger houses. When this card is found upright in a reading it is not intended as a temporary recommendation, until something better comes along.

This is a very positive card, one of the best in a deck, and that brings me to another point. You would hardly need this card to tell you that your life is as you dreamed it would be, so that leaves anticipation and still living in hope that one day it will come true. But we are left with yet one more possibility. Maybe someone needs to take a look around and see what they do have.

REVERSED

When this card is found reversed, dissatisfaction is tearing apart one's world, and will continually block their path to fulfillment. One may possibly be feeling trapped and unaware in a never-ending cycle of thinking, *this is it?* only to fixate on trivial flaws or perceived inadequacies and continuing the hunt for a replacement.

Perfect is a word used to describe the simply obtainable, such as not spilling your coffee while you walk. It can also be used as a target to motivate one toward higher achievement, but when one judges others in their entirety with such a standard, there will never be anyone or anything good enough. This concept is never limited to a single aspect of one's life. The standards of satisfaction in one's life are often that person's current state of perception of all matters.

As you may notice, this card reversed goes beyond a single situation to represent a pattern of behavior. Of course someone can find themselves in a bad relationship or job, but this card reversed represents one's overall perception of all matters in their life, and when there is disillusionment, despondency, or dissatisfaction it will appear.

It can be said by some that this represents cracks in the dream brought about by external forces, but I see that as unlikely since the overall premise of this card is based on one's expectations and comparing it to the reality. There are no two people with the same dream and since everything is relative it becomes a matter of passing judgment on the elements that make up one's life. Then questions arise within of whether this is good enough for them.

This card upright and reversed often comes down to the perceptions and expectations of the person the reading is for. Their goals and aspirations were formed by them and they are the only one able to measure their success by their own standard. One may alter their dream as they see fit, but others cannot affect it adversely unless one allows them that power. There are both obstacles and impassable blocks, and they are entirely different. The former comes from the external and the latter is created internally by the one with the dream.

It is also important to remember that the people that are part of your dream have dreams of their own. The elements of one's dreams that involve relationships with others must be symbiotic and if one destroys another's dream in selfishness, they will surely attempt to return the favor.

Ace of Swords

UPRIGHT

When this card appears in a reading, it primarily represents thoughts, but of course, that is too vague to be of much good to anyone. Or is it? Our minds are constantly at work, formulating ideas, evaluating decisions, and thinking about what we are going to do next. However, one shouldn't have a difficult time connecting this card to the important thoughts that are either at the forefront or lingering at the mental peripheral when other thoughts need attention. That is how we experience thinking about grand plans for the future, or ideas that are being formed to lead us toward a goal. Before one can physically move forward along their path, they must first see it in their mind.

Communication can be an added or a stand-alone possibility here, since ideas, as well as thoughts, can be exchanged with others for a number of different reasons. Sharing an idea with others for the purpose of obtaining useful feedback might be something to consider, as well as collaborating in partnership to achieve a mutual goal.

Aces are beginnings, and you will likely notice me mentioning that again with the other Aces, as a reminder. In the case of this card, we are looking at the beginning of ideas or plans. One should consider inspirational moments here as well, as they are the birth, or seed of a new idea.

When this card appears it may indicate a need to open the lines of communication, as there may be someone with information that is important. One can also derive from this a need to keep an open mind about the opinions of others, and allow them to understand, support, and enlighten. A possibility that should be considered in light of what I have expressed here, is how people communicate with themselves. Some of us have exceptional memories, but keeping all the details of an idea or plan contained within the mind can leave some things to chance.

Keeping a written or digital record of various thoughts and ideas does more than help one remember, it also allows one to better exchange information within. We tend to think we are objective about our thoughts, but that isn't always the case. Comparing a thought from a week or a month ago may yield a different perspective within the dynamic of a new day.

REVERSED

Communication begins with the thoughts and ideas one wishes to express, and if they have not been well thought out or are ill conceived, then the ensuing back and forth of words will not likely be productive. There really isn't such a thing as bad communication, anymore than a computer is responsible for what one reads on the screen. The formation of what one wishes to express takes place within, as does the decision to communicate the thought.

There are things that are better left unsaid, and in this card reversed, one will often find that out, after the fact. It could be referred to as bad communication if one wishes, but communicating a bad thought is actually more accurate. What one says is only as good as what one thinks before they speak.

The element of miscommunication that may apply would be on the receiving end where someone is not actively listening to what is being expressed to them, and someone does not hear, or misunderstands what is being communicated. This is found in times where one's mind is focusing on what they want to say when they get an opportunity, and not on what they are hearing.

In this era of advanced communication technology, there are many ways to express ideas, and people now spend time typing, reading, then typing again, and so on. It would seem this would make things clearer and less likely to be misunderstood. However, what is lost in digital communication is a person's intent when speaking, and reaction when listening. These are revealed in body language and facial expressions, and are more important to sharing information than some people realize.

Interpreting this card reversed as bad, or miscommunication, is fine as long as one realizes that it covers far more than just sound waves traveling through the air from one person's mouth to another person's ear.

Another possibility here is intentionally hurtful expressions toward another, where one thought and then decided to inflict pain or fear upon someone using some form of communication. Their reasons are of course important to the situation, but they are not described in this reversed card alone.

Perhaps something was digitally expressed by someone that seemed inappropriate, but without the reveal of intent, one only assumes they are serious. I guess a smiley emoticon could help. Then again, maybe it just furthers the interpretation of this card, whereas what was relayed still hurts anyway.

Two of Swords

UPRIGHT

This is most often stagnating in conflict, either internal or external, where progress is blocked, and in a word, impasse. This card may also reflect an avoidance of opportunity out of fear or uncertainty, as one has lived with indecision long enough for it to be a habit. Putting off a decision is in fact a decision in itself, whether it is in connection to a situation where one must choose between two acts, and it becomes a third option, or *an act* or *don't act* decision where it defaults to *don't take any* action.

One should evaluate the situation and not presume that they are better off choosing to be indecisive, since whatever the question is that lies at the heart of the decision did manage to get their interest. If it did not, there probably wouldn't be a choice to make.

Given its association with the suit of Swords, it is likely that this card is a conflict of thought, ideas, or ideals, where one is being challenged by preconceptions, expectations, or a predisposition when faced with a possible opportunity. As I mentioned, the appearance of this card does often refer to a lack of progress, but that does not always have to be the case.

Something else that can be represented here is passive-aggressive behavior where one propels themselves by appearing to give decisions away to others. The genius of passive manipulation, if I dare refer to it that way, is one being able to fulfill their desires without having to share responsibility or risk consequences. It may be clever, but it is destructive to relationships in its dishonesty alone, and it will eventually be revealed.

The key element here is indecisiveness, and one may not have to look very deep to realize that, but it is only a symptom, with the cause or purpose at the heart of the situation. Events of the past play a role in the decisions one makes, and attempts to avoid repeating mistakes are strong influences.

We learn everything by comparison, and I do mean everything. It is the basis of our development as members of our species, and this is why we might fear the unknown; there is nothing yet in our mind to compare it to and determine whether it is good or bad.

We are also gifted with giving the benefit of the doubt and therein lies a common conflict that leads to indecisiveness. Prior heartbreaks and unwanted outcomes are being compared to the current situation, and one's destiny is somewhere on the other side.

REVERSED

When one reaches a conclusion, by comparison, and determines that a choice is worth the risk, or it is not, then proceeds to act decisively, they have realized the primary interpretation of this card reversed. There should be an accompanying feeling of confidence in the decision once made, and although it is yet to be validated as correct, both risk and reward have been carefully evaluated and accepted.

Many situations have far too much ambiguity and uncertainty attached for one to believe they can navigate their path on correct decisions alone. A decision can only be as good as the information available when they reach the time when it needs to be made.

The lament, *if only I knew then what I know now* is the basis of a lesson learned, or it should be.

As I described in the upright description of this card, indecisiveness is actually inserting a third choice into the decision or defaulting to a doing nothing position as the result of not acting. One will not find the presence of either of the aforementioned possibilities here, nor will they find any evidence of deferring the decision to another person. That means responsibility has been accepted and progress is made through an honest approach with others, and/or with oneself.

One might consider that the stress associated with some decisions may lie more in the commitment to it than the outcome. Only the one who faces the decision can fully grasp how it affects them, and one simply cannot achieve their goals or find fulfillment and practice decision avoidance at the same time. We make so many decisions every day that we stop paying attention to them, until one of those decisions leads us to a choice where there is uncertainty or an unknown outcome. At that point, we stop, now consciously aware that we do not have enough information to decide.

Think of a time when one was entertaining the idea of trying something new for dinner. Most of us will ask someone else to relate information or a past experience with the meal. What does one decide if the response is negative, even though everybody's tastes are different? That is a pretty simple decision with more often than not very little in the way of consequences. However, that decision was given away to another, and what happens to bigger decisions? In this card reversed, one accepts them, and makes them.

Three of Swords

UPRIGHT

Primarily associated with the heartache of betrayal, this card is also expandable to other various situations that could lead to heartache. This could include the disintegration of a long-distance romance, even if there is no actual infidelity or betrayal. Further, it could reflect disenchantment and even unrequited love. Many of us believe the most painful thing one can experience is a broken heart, and because of that, this card can inflict symptoms of the very thing one fears the most. Yes, it does describe matters of the heart in a way that could possibly be a harbinger of an end, such as a separation or divorce. However, it does not define an ending with absolute certainty.

Providing true solace with my words might be a lot for me to expect, but expectations are what bring us down, and the very thing that picks us back up. Relationships are built, destroyed, and then overcome on that very sentiment – how we see things happening.

Regardless of our social connections, we each move through life as individuals. The strength of commonalities can bring us together as couples when two paths converge, and what happens in the time after that is based on expectations – two different sets of expectations. Viewing two paths now as one is an illusion, and that statement may seem unromantic, but it is the truth of a relationship where both partners respect the other's expectations. To believe there is now only one path means somebody gave up theirs for the other.

This card depicts something unwanted by at least one of the partners, but even if the event it represents seems sudden or surprising, it may very well not be entirely unexpected. It is one's hopes and expectations evolving into stubborn perceptions when the situation involves disenchantment and unrequited love: a convergence of paths that took place only in the mind, and it often results in perpetual heartache temporarily hidden by denial.

When this card appears in a reading, one should honestly examine their expectations and compare them to their partners. From there, one should realize that their path is still intact and the only reality is whether or not they can continue side by side or the divergence is inevitable. It may not be as bad as it seems if one is willing to look closely at the situation.

REVERSED

There is an interesting paradox when this card appears reversed. It almost seems it has to follow the appearance of itself upright to make any sense in a reading. Granted there are other cards that can precede this card reversed to reference such aspects as making up after a fight, but this is generally a following card when it appears this way. It is difficult to reconcile in a relationship when you didn't know you broke up. If by timing a reading was not done that revealed the point of divergence or conflict, this card's appearance reversed should still not lay before the unaware. Other cards when reversed are like this one in that they often describe aftermath situations of known events. The resolution represented here can be of forgiveness, or clarity of a previous misunderstanding.

There are actually a multitude of possibilities that could lead to a mutually agreed upon decision to continue on together, and the best interpretation here may be simply two people mending fences and getting back together. Then in context of the situation, perhaps this is an indicator that it is time to take the initiative and move things in that direction.

It is not uncommon for cards upright and reversed to offer appropriate action yet to be taken toward the desired goal. There is no presumption here that one wants to reconcile, since a question was asked and this card reversed is part of the answer. The cards do not provide suggestions as alternatives.

If communication has broken down in a relationship while both parties wait, unsure, afraid, or angry, for the other to act first, then you will have an opportunity missed and the outcome can change. Just as the situations described in the appearance of this card upright are affected by expectations, so too are they significant here. Thoughts of who should act first generate expectations that further diverge the two paths, and if that is what one truly wants, then what exactly is the decision they are trying to make?

One final aspect to consider here is the passage of time after a relationship has ended. Though slightly contrary to what I have previously stated about the appearance of this card not likely coming out of nowhere, it can reflect a rekindling of a relationship that was long since thought to be over.

Four of Swords

UPRIGHT

Life can come at us pretty fast and furious sometimes and after awhile weariness can insist on rest and replenishment. As much as one would like to remain in a state of constant forward motion, the mind and body will just not cooperate. In this card, we have a representation of time needed or taken to clear thoughts and reenergize the body. In context one can determine if it is a choice to be made or will be forced upon them in time.

This isn't about sleep, although it could play a role; it is about slowing down for awhile and redirecting energies away from areas in one's life that may contain high levels of stress. It may involve an evaluation of circumstances by taking the pressure off, or regaining balance and broadening one's focus. As the expression goes, *one cannot always see the forest for the trees*, and stepping back can provide a new perspective and understanding on how to proceed.

Does one always realize when they reach a point of diminishing returns in their efforts to achieve an objective? If this threshold is missed, one's progress will eventually be negated completely and frustration will become the mindset of action. Some of us can be quite driven, and as well many may display grace under pressure, but even so, everyone of us have our limits, and beyond that, what about health, balance, and harmony in one's life?

A possibility to consider when this card appears is that one just needs a vacation or a weekend away. Being wise means knowing one's limitations, and taking a temporary retreat or exile is not giving up.

I have always liked the expression *you can't get there from here* because it can never be true. If one can actually get there at all, they can get there from anywhere. Even if you have to start over and choose a different route, you will eventually get there from the place previously known as *here*. Looking at it from a less physical perspective where the word *there* represents happiness and fulfillment, or the achievement of a goal, and the word *here* represents a current state of mind, it applies just as equally.

The actual point of the statement is that one may need to choose and define a different route, as in start anew, not necessarily from the beginning, but with new perspective. It is that very sentiment that the interpretation of this card describes and what it takes to get a fresh start is the highest consideration.

REVERSED

When this card appears reversed it marks the reawakening of the spirit and recovery from near depletion. It is finding the new route, the overcoming of obstacles, and making progress upon the path toward the goal. Situations should look different now and the process will be clearer.

Positive actions come from positive thoughts and a promising outlook. One shouldn't need a Tarot card to tell them that they are feeling reenergized, but a card can tell them that they soon will be, if they aren't as yet, and now is the time to get back into action. Sometimes we choose detachment or isolation to heal emotional wounds, and sometimes it is chosen for us due to overwhelming circumstances, but one should now consider that part of the past and get back into the world.

This should not be thought of as urging one to plunge headlong back into a situation under the belief that everything will just fall into place for them. If one has not already taken the opportunity to look at the situation with their new mindset, that should be a high priority. Taking the time to step back, rest, and recover, for the purpose of retaining good health, and maintaining balance and harmony in one's life, should naturally lead to a good look at the situations in one's life.

It isn't an absolute that one's previous approach wasn't working, but it would certainly seem important to know one way or the other. With consideration for the possibility that one's respite may not have been so much a choice, but rather a need due to weariness, I think that makes the point obvious.

Aside from pointing toward the occurrence of a reawakening, renewed outlook, and refreshed spirit in one's life, this card reversed could also serve as notice that it is time to get back to work, as I previously mentioned. This deserves a little more attention since taking the pressure off can come to feel comfortable, and it may have become too comfortable. When applying this to having isolated oneself in order to recover from emotional setbacks it is possible that levels of social anxiety may have taken hold, and the desire to resume progress is being suppressed. There is not always a direct connection between being ready to start anew and being able to begin. Each situation is unique and this card reversed may signify that it is time.

Five of Sword

UPRIGHT

The interpretation of this card starts with defeat, and can possibly reach dishonor and humiliation. The reality here is only defeat, as it is in the behavior of others that honor becomes dishonor if one stays true to their belief, or noble cause, in their heart.

One cannot realistically expect to win all battles or overcome all odds, so to feel humiliated comes from another source. Did one truly give their best effort? Is one now being portrayed as a coward because they chose not to succumb to provocation? The answers to these questions should be considered when one is being tormented internally by feelings of inadequacy, shame, or humiliation. There are times when the sacrifice of one's pride is the best action to take. Suffering one's pride can be a very difficult choice to make, and there certainly is not a shortage of people willing to exploit that fact in others to raise their own feelings of self worth. In a literal sense, bruises on the body are preferred to bruises to the ego.

We place a lot, if not everything on what others think about us, and to that end we can let our perceptions of ourselves become that which we imagine others to have. In this situation, it points to a loss in one's self worth, an emotional wound that leads one down a path that they would not normally take, and this is an important element when considering this card in a reading.

Fearing embarrassment or humiliation as certain events unfold changes one's mindset as a moment approaches where a decision will be made. If one successfully navigates the situation by not allowing pride to take control over their behavior, they may have to contend with feelings in the aftermath that can influence subsequent actions.

The interpretation of this card on the surface is defeat, but defeat of what? Which comes first, conflict or humiliation? One is likely to discover that humiliation always precedes conflict, even if it appears the other way around in one's perception of the situation.

In rising to the defense of another for the sake of honor, one is inserting their pride into the situation, and it may very well be noble and warranted. Then again, it could be self-serving, as an opportunity to enhance how one believes others see them. I am not saying one should not defend their friend or ally; I am simply raising the question of one's motivation.

REVERSED

Elements of restitution and making amends for prior deeds should be considered when interpreting this card reversed. This relates directly to actions taken in defense of one's pride, and the affects one's decisions had on others. There is also the possibility that one has seen through the fog generated by the risk to their pride and taken appropriate and prudent action. One could look for an overall victory in the outcome due to restraint and self-control in the face of provocation.

In the end, acts prompted by impressions of justification may only have appeared to be proper choices, and, in the case of this card reversed, one has realized the greater honor in letting things pass. A willingness to sacrifice one's pride takes great strength, and it is truly more rewarding in the overall picture. The values of those that view restraint in the face of provocation and humiliation as a weakness are not likely to be a reliable source of good judgment. Being encouraged to respond at the level the challenge is made increases the need for strength and often adds another layer of conflict to the situation.

When this card appears reversed one has made the right choice, or response to the circumstances, and this may very well lead to environmental changes that are the results of a change in perspective, either in the one, others involved, or both. Seeing oneself and others in a different light is an aspect here that is actually unavoidable, since making what might be the less popular choice is usually quite revealing.

The element of inner strength that is present here can reflect one's strength of conviction emanating from their foundation of beliefs or personal philosophies. The possibilities here can be a realization of the correct choice, either before or after, or total restraint and control in the face of conflict.

As I have described, there is a reference to defeat in this card upright, but after further examination it should be seen as a catalectic event more than the actual interpretation. Defeat, whether it is perceived or realized, points us toward pride, and the role it plays in one's decision-making.

Six of Swords

UPRIGHT

Sometimes we cannot go it alone when things are difficult. The support of another, even if it is only the knowledge that they are nearby and willing if we need them, can be a difference maker. There are no absolutes on who the benevolent friend is or even if they are another human being. As children there were often pets that faithfully stood by us and saw us through troubling times, and there is no reason to exclude that possibility in adult situations.

The interpretation of this card is broad enough to include anyone or anything that is there for us and helps us find our way through to better times. If one is experiencing difficult times, they should take comfort in such an entity, and in that regard this card can also serve as notice that one is in need and there is somebody who would like to help. There are also no limits on what one might constitute a need for healing in the situation. As well as the possibility of emotionally troubling times, a recovery from a physical ailment or an affliction could also be represented here.

The primary element of this card is a need for assistance, recognized or not, and that one is not alone and should not choose to be suffering entirely within. Loneliness fosters uncertainty about the future, and one's expectations about what will happen are a weight that makes the burden seem greater. I am relatively sure this isn't a great revelation to most, but it is the emphasis of this card when it appears in a reading, and that makes it something to consider in the current situation.

As described, this helpful entity could have many different forms and assist one in many situations, even without conscious awareness. Looking deeper into the situation, we can expand this benevolent entity even beyond living things, and also discover a further purpose for their presence. Another aspect of this card is protection and that might be described as a guardian angel, the spirit of a deceased relative or friend, and perhaps a structure of belief that provides someone to whom one can talk.

One can conclude here that things will get better if they are difficult now, and there is somebody nearby that can be looked to for support if one is willing. Dependence is not a weakness unless one chooses to let go and live by what it provides alone, and it becomes an absolute dependency. From time to time people do need someone or something to be there for them, and as well, sometimes others may need you.

REVERSED

Some of us may be familiar with a dream, a nightmare if you prefer, in which you need to run to avert a crisis and try as you might, you cannot move. You can feel the frustration as your legs will not move at the speed you know they can. It's as if they are made of lead. The situation progresses toward a tragic end as helplessness and hopelessness overcome you and then you wake up. In the aftermath, you lay there processing the transition from dream to reality and the paralysis seems to remain for a few moments, retaining the helpless feeling with it. What applies to the interpretation of this card reversed is the often-lost feeling in the dream that you were the only one that could act. There are often others in the dream who seem oblivious to the crisis, as if you were the only one that cared.

Have you actually convinced your conscious mind that you are truly alone and the only one capable of seeing you through the current difficult situation? Feelings of helplessness and being alone are evident in this situation, and although it doesn't seem like there is a choice, there truly is one to be made. The farther inside one crawls, the harder it is to climb out.

At this point, I haven't specifically described a difference between the upright and reversed interpretation of this card, but that is defined by how much farther one has fallen, alone. This is not moving away from difficult times; this is moving toward them, into worse situations by not acknowledging someone willing, or flat out refusing, an offer of support. These are the escalating effects of going it alone. This card reversed can be expanded to include an attempt to completely ignore the situation in the misguided belief that it will resolve itself.

The reference to the dream also provides something else one must come to realize. If something is troubling one, it may with persistent effort be pushed from the conscious mind, but denial does not clear the unconscious mind, and we act upon unconscious thoughts more frequently than we, of course, are consciously aware of.

Attempting to ignore feelings, such as guilt, can lead to self-sabotage, and if one has accepted that there is nothing they can do in a particular situation, their feelings of powerlessness will easily spread to other areas of their life. Taking oneself out of a situation mentally isn't resolving anything, and is sure to make matters worse.

Seven of Swords

UPRIGHT

The expression *circumvention of conventional rules* is truly the best way to explain the situation. The reason is that it leaves intent ambiguous, and that is an important element of this card. It can be meant to depict theft for profit or that there are no other means of survival available.

Placing judgment on the actions of another is often done by a simplification of what is right or wrong, but this is possibly a situation that falls into a gray area where the *why* should be considered as well. I am not myself deciding right or wrong or even condoning gray area deception. At the same time, I am not prescribing rigidity to authoritative or socialized rules. I am describing the meaning of this card.

If one feels they have been put at a disadvantage by prior events, they may see limited choices to overcome them or even survive. This can easily slip into thoughts of getting even or revenge, whereas the gray area really might not be so gray after all. Expanding from that, it becomes apparent that right or wrong by the standards of others isn't the value considered by the person that this card speaks about. The significance lies in what they think is the right thing to do to serve themselves or their purpose.

The appearance of this card can represent different forms of deception, for example, falsehoods or misleading others by omission. This may as well serve the noble purpose of protecting someone deserving, and then again it may protect a selfish interest or a damaging secret. The question is how to tell the difference between the potentially understandable, or self-serving acts of deceit. The answer to that will always come back to the situation, the strength of the question that one has asked of the cards.

One more aspect to consider is that, by itself, this card does not directly depict who has initiated the deception, or for that matter, if others are involved. Furthermore, Tarot card readings are not evidence, only insight. If they create awareness and healthy skepticism, that is one thing, but when they generate suspicion and accusations, then that is another matter entirely. One must always consider what purpose is served by confronting another with suspicions.

REVERSED

The significant aspects to consider when this card is found reversed are the exposure of deception and attempts to make something right. How amends are provided, achieved, or realized can be a more complex matter. If one has used deception to serve a purpose they viewed as noble, they themselves in good conscience will likely attempt to restore things as they were, or right a wrong to the best of their ability. Someone who has served only their own desires by subterfuge is likely to be caught or exposed, and they have no choice but to make restitution and amends. The interpretation here runs deep enough to include investigations, surveillance, and may as well be a representation of revenge.

The egregiousness of deception is always a matter of point of view, and that applies to both sides of any situation. Is deception by omission as bad as a blatant lie? The honest answer is that there isn't enough information in that statement to decide. When you see only one side of the story, you move from neutrality into bias. The point here is that this card reversed describes a significant event in the aftermath of a previous event, known or unknown. So the question becomes, is one looking for a resolution, a mea culpa, Karma, payback, or any combination of these.

Referring back to my assertion of deception exposed and making things right, this should represent a conclusion to a situation, but as all events offer choices, all aspects should be considered. One must know the truth of why they decided to do a reading in the first place, and what one expects to learn from the cards.

If the position of this card reversed in a reading represents the person the reading is for, then it is likely to be describing it's time to come clean and face the music. The value of one choosing to make things right weighed against unintended exposure and then followed by repentance should determine a reasonable resolution.

A correct interpretation of this card can be blocked by denial, and then on the other hand lead to aspersive behavior depending on which side the querent is standing on. As events unfold remember the Tarot cards do not make the decisions, and they should not be used to deflect responsibility if a choice is followed by regret.

Eight of Swords

UPRIGHT

Some of us, perhaps many of us, at one time or another have felt trapped in a situation or relationship. In some cases, one might see few if any alternatives and teeter on resignation, followed by despair and feelings of hopelessness. The interpretation of this card is centered on one feeling trapped somewhere or with someone and feeling powerless to affect change. It can describe simple moments or events and can expand to include jobs or personal relationships.

What must be considered here is the distinct difference between feeling powerless and being powerless. Granted there are certain situations where one is legitimately unable to effect change on their condition, but more often than not, it is the lack of will that cages one, and that is the meaning here. The bars of these cages may be made of many things, some of which might be guilt, fear of going it alone, or a belief that things will improve on their own in time.

The latter is the equivalent of acceptance and that equals resignation.

When one chooses to do absolutely nothing, they are relinquishing control of their life and giving it to another. If one has found themselves at this point already, whatever the circumstances, what are the chances that capitulating will result in an improvement in the situation? A person's happiness is enhanced by others, never defined, and to give that power to another is to become an object of their desires, at the sacrifice of one's own. It really seems obvious until you cloud it with emotions and introduce denial.

You are likely to notice some aspects of the Tarot cards in general that I redundantly point to, and here is one of them. It seems unlikely that one would need a Tarot card to tell them that they feel trapped, and possibly oppressed in a relationship or situation. As the cards are not going to tell one what they want to hear, they also do not serve as affirmers. If the appearance of this card applies to the one asking the question within the context of the reading, then it should be interpreted as the shattering of acceptance and the piercing of the denial bubble.

Furthermore, if such a situation currently exists, it might very well have influenced the question in the first place. The most important thing to take away from this is not necessarily to end a relationship or situation, but to abandon or avoid a passive approach.

REVERSED

When someone is in a situation they feel they do not want to be in, they need to see it clearly and face it to make a change. This awareness, and the will to change, is the representation found in this card reversed. Breaking free and moving on is not an absolute of this card, although it is a possibility. What matters the most here is one reclaiming their control over what happens in their future and actively pursuing what they want in life.

There may very well be others in one's life that truly have good intentions, but regardless of how well the others understand, they simply cannot follow one's heart for them. Beyond that it can get much worse if the situation involves another who is selfish and acts in their own best interest, keeping one down to further their own desires. The value of one's need to be in control of their own decisions cannot be overstated, as things are often more complex than they seem if one just glances at them. Consider a situation where one is being encouraged to leave a relationship, perhaps even pulled away from it by trusted others. The others do not have to navigate the emotionally charged waters the one does, and having one's best interest at heart notwithstanding, it is still a matter of giving away an important decision.

It is not possible for me or the Tarot cards to decide which is right either, and then, once again, that would still be allowing another the power to make the choice. The destiny that belongs to the one cannot be found if the one does not make the decisions. The interpretation here is not which of the others involved wins a tug of war over what is the best thing for the one in question. There may be difficult decisions to be made, and the ability to see them, understand them, and make them, is the message in this card reversed.

It is not necessary to leave a situation or relationship to make a fresh start. The new beginning takes place inside one and what it entails and who it involves is a decision that can only be made by the one upon the path. When a Tarot reading is done, it is directed at the one individual who holds the question in their heart. Contained in the context of the reading will be insight, not advice or influence, and the ability to see that very concept is to understand the meaning here.

Nine of Swords

UPRIGHT

Close your eyes and attempt to fall asleep, if you dare. That might be a sentiment going through one's mind when this card appears. Elements to consider would be dread of upcoming events and anxiety over aspects of the current situation. The bad things that could happen often cross the bridge of *what if* to become the thing that will happen with a little help from one's imagination.

Some of us are quite proficient at tormenting ourselves over possibilities, and can rationalize our worries and anxiety as just being ready for the worst possible outcome. The ability to sleep, and return to sleep once awakened, is a symptom of a mind focusing on life changing events that will deprive one of something. The fear of loss is the greatest fear we all face.

The conscious mind processes pertinent information, points of focus, and allows the ability to suppress thoughts, with or without conscious awareness that this is happening. The unconscious mind on the other hand, will resist this suppression, and forces strong thoughts back to awareness, sometimes creating elaborate and cryptic vignettes for one to view while the conscious mind is shut down. It is not that you are being shown the certain future, but, instead, the potential negative outcomes one is trying not to think about. What this describes is that worry and anxiety can exist on both the conscious and unconscious levels, and this does not indicate that it is unavoidable, but instead that one is repressing the feelings, not facing them. Stop me if you have heard this before. *Worrying about the future never changes how it unfolds.*

Other elements to consider in the interpretation of this card are feelings of guilt and regret. Sleepless nights and mental distractions can be a by-product of one having done something, or caused something to happen that they now wish they had not. The representation in this card can refer to both the inadvertent results of words or actions, or regrettable behavior that is now about to be revealed and effect them adversely.

The heart of the interpretation of this card is that one is troubled or suffering in the present about events of the future or the past. One more aspect to consider involving the possibility of regret is that one might be now contemplating action that will result in feelings of lament in the future.

REVERSED

From coming to terms with one's previous actions to surviving unfounded distress, the interpretation of this card when reversed can cover a lot of ground. One can look to more restful nights along with feelings of comfort and relief as indicators of the representation here. It is possible that one will discover that they have worried for nothing when the outcome is realized, but as well, one can also think their way through it before the event occurs.

This is overcoming the dread and anxiety with a rational and realistic evaluation of what it is one actually fears. There is a certain amount of exaggerated and unfounded feelings inherent in this card, upright and reversed, and that one is now aware of this is the primary key here. From that, it is possible that this card represents a lesson going forward. Anxiety and worry can be detrimental to one's health and, as stated, have no real value toward the outcome, and that certainly sounds like an important lesson to me.

On matters regarding guilt and regret, this quite often requires more than just thinking about it, and approaching others that are involved is likely a necessary step revealed in this card reversed. This would point to someone else's ability or willingness to accept a situation in order to find comfort and relief. If one were to believe otherwise, it is highly unlikely that they are interpreting this card correctly as one's feelings of regret and guilt will still be suppressed without the other's involvement, and this is instead a representation of resolution in a situation.

One is sure to experience a spiritual healing and an overall improvement in their outlook, not to mention feeling more rested. When one discovers this card, there has been a comparison based on acceptance in one's life. Having accepted potential catastrophic outcomes as surmountable in the past, they have now accepted an outcome that was survivable and likely far less devastating than they had imagined.

Is it possible that something bad really did happen? Perhaps, but even so, by comparison, it was not the end of the world they envisioned. The obvious focus here is what the mind can imagine to cause worry, anxiety, and regret, and the ability to move through it, survive it, and overcome it, to feel better tomorrow.

Ten of Swords

UPRIGHT

First the bad news; this is as bad as one *thinks* it can possibly get. The good news, this is as bad as one thinks it can possibly get. Yes, those statements are identical, except for one thing, the emphasis on the word *thinks*. It may not offer much consolation in the aftermath of a perceived catastrophic event, but I am not aware of any case where things really could not get worse.

There are many possibilities that can only be relative to someone and their situation, and how bad something is depends on their perceptions and expectations. I am not trying to describe an event or situation represented by this card as being insignificant – that is for one to decide on their own – but I am going to point out that this does not mean the end of the world. Interpreting this card as total devastation and ruin in one's life is not getting the message.

Embracing disappointment or a single event that doesn't go one's way, thereby allowing it to infest other areas of their life, then yes, things will get worse. However, this card is not telling anyone it will get worse. It is warning one to contain the negative feelings, or metaphorically speaking, to stop the bleeding.

Personally, I only associate the appearance of this card with undesired outcomes, as in blocked progress or resistance, not as a devastating setback that causes one to start over with nothing. You will notice that I make mention of the paradox inherent to Tarot cards from time to time, where one chooses by expectation to find what the cards are warning one to avoid. That applies here. One should only view the cards that appear in a reading as obstacles to avoid or overcome, or as depicting a clear path toward the desired outcome. There are not any absolutes in a reading, only possibilities.

Any decision can alter the path, and if this card does appear, it would be truly devastating to resign oneself to a feeling of inevitable tragedy. Therein lies the rub, or the paradox, or the self-fulfilling prophecy, what have you. The elements associated with this card are related to what one will feel in such an event or situation. To be blunt, the cards will not tell one they are doomed, ever, but one may feel that way, and the best interpretation here is that if one cannot avoid the situation, don't make it worse.

REVERSED

When this card is found reversed it represents a determined, if not positive outlook in the wake of a devastating event. One cannot look positively toward the future while trying to remove the tragic event from their history, and simultaneously repeating *if only*. Such an event can shape one's life; it will remain part of their history, and the only thing they can do is accept it and maintain control of how it affects their outlook. This may be a new beginning, but there is not anything here about starting over with nothing or having lost all of one's progress along their path.

There are too many intersecting paths for one to have a realistic belief that everything will always fall into place for them. One's future depends on how they respond when they endure undesired outcomes. This card reversed can represent vindication in a situation where a bad outcome was unfairly imposed on someone, and sincere efforts are being made to restore matters to their original form.

A consistent element that must always be included is one's personal involvement in how the situation progresses. However, there are not any recriminations, vengeance, or retribution here; it represents a positive approach to negative circumstances, resulting in one making progress once again. Another possibility is avoidance of a tragic event, but it still requires one's participation and awareness of potential consequences, and should not be attributed to just a lucky break. The primary focus here is a before and after outlook where one is not fixing blame upon themselves or others, and what brought them to the brink of hopelessness has been understood, accepted, and is now behind them.

There should be a reinvigoration of spirit and renewed hope, brought about by a lesson learned about oneself. Growth applies to this card reversed by evaluation of one's inner strength now that it has been put to the test. Even though it sounds quite cliché, one should walk away from a bad situation a better person, and the interpretation here should be deeper than recovery. Recognizing the event or situation represented here should not be difficult, but determining what it means to one will take introspection.

Ace of Wands

UPRIGHT

Fire is synonymous with passion and drive, and it begins when the spark of desire meets opportunity, and that is the primary consideration here. This is something that is beginning to burn inside one, and although the spark may have already been there, it is about to fully ignite. There are unlimited possibilities here and each individual will have to determine to what it refers, but it should not be difficult because the desire will be strong. There is an interesting correlation between choices and desires, in that we often choose what we desire, yet there are times where the choice results in a desire. Either way, sooner or later our passions will define us.

It is indeterminable why we have the desires we have – perhaps past lives, grand design, or childhood influences – but I believe that the mystery need not be solved, just accepted, and it is our destiny to embrace our passion. However, the balance of risk versus reward one weighs will be affected as the strength of the passion grows and drives one further down the path toward their goals, and if sound reasoning is not maintained, it is possible to become blinded by ambition.

Such elements as inspiration and intuition will apply to the interpretation of this card in a reading. The question of whether something reaches out to the mind and inspires one, or the mind reaches out for possibilities in some ethereal, supernatural way is part of the mystery, but when the drive is powerful, one will certainly be inspired in some way.

Although it is not necessary to understand why we have such feelings of passions, it is beneficial for one to understand that they have them, and specifically that they are truly their own. I personally have embraced the passions of others because I cared about them and their interests. However, I did not make this choice at the expense of my own passions. Sharing interests and desires are certain to make a relationship stronger, but it is important to maintain a situation where the passionate energy moves in both directions.

People often find themselves locked in an internal struggle over fitting in with others and asserting oneself as a unique individual. Passion is the difference maker we already possess and should point us toward others who have similar desires, and to be unique is to embrace and follow our own feelings, not change them to suit others.

REVERSED

Feeling dispassionate is one possibility here, but the Four of Cups really covers such feelings more specifically. What actually works better here is an overbearing passionate approach to other people and situations. Statements intended to incite, provoke, and control the actions of others to serve one's own ends would be identifiable elements of this card reversed. One's pattern of behavior could be causing others to act irresponsibly to shield one from possible consequences. Maintaining the balance between acting passionately and acting appropriately can be circumvented by influencing others to do their evil bidding, so to speak. Remember, of course, this is still a representation of a beginning.

In the upright description of this card, I described how one's desires and passions are their own to find on their own, but there is within many people a susceptibility to the passions of others. One can recognize these people within the thralls of religion, cults, and even crowds. What these have in common is a passionate, if not overzealous, leadership who by word or action ignites and controls the passions of people. Whether to be perceived by others as malevolent or benevolent, it amounts to one playing the role of puppet master over the desires of another.

Now as bad as I make that sound, in some circumstances it might not be; however, if this card appears reversed then there is in fact something wrong in the situation. One could possibly be on either side of the situation. For the interpretation of this card reversed, one should look at how someone's passions are not being properly influenced or respected in a current situation, such as, leading or being led by desires involved with loneliness and a need for acceptance, where one's passions are exploited to fulfill the very same need in others. There may be both positive and negative reinforcements, in dangled carrots and/or blustering and threats. These elements will present an obstacle to progress, with this reversed card referring to either a singular event or an ongoing resistance, perhaps described as a spider's web in which one is trapped.

Another possibility that can stand entirely on its own is a passion in the form of a grudge, where one is consumed with revenge and is destroying themselves and everyone around them in pursuit of a vendetta.

Two of Wands

UPRIGHT

The early stages of success, or potential success for that matter, foster the desire to act and do something. Impatience might be present in this situation, but it is not entirely an unwillingness to wait in the moment; it is an all-encompassing feeling of not doing all that one can to make progress.

One may choose to interpret this card as a crossroads in a business endeavor, or perhaps a point of readying oneself for some yet unseen event. The metaphorical reference of being at a crossroads implies choosing between two different directions, but it might as well refer to deciding between a time to plan and a time to act. Planning and making decisions is actually taking action and if the correct decisions are made it represents progress.

What defines this card is the discovery of the truth in what I just stated. Action begins when one contemplates the possible results of various choices they face regarding what action to take. Proper planning and preparation reveals the best action to take and the process chosen is then more efficient. This seems obvious enough, but then again the weight of one's dreams upon one's shoulders raises the stakes and may lead to confusing expeditiousness with effectiveness.

Possibly further exacerbating one's impatience is the practice of visualization, which is mentally living in the success one has yet to achieve. And by no means am I rejecting this, quite the contrary. However, when doing so, the perceived results may seem closer than they are in reality. Is this card telling one to slow down? Perhaps, but more importantly it is speaking of knowing when to slow down.

Among the words I have chosen to offer in abundance within this text are *evaluate* and *expectations*. By applying the former to the latter, combined with where one currently is on the path toward their goal, then one has grasped the message in this card. If one expects to arrive at an intended destination, then one must know precisely where they are currently. Chances are pretty good my previous statement was understood before you read it, but when the objective is less tangible than say grandmother's house or a hotel on the beach, then the ability to realize where you are upon your path toward your dream isn't nearly as simple.

REVERSED

Being caught off guard is a clear indicator of having failed to prepare, and when this card appears reversed, an obstinate attitude is the likely starting point. Choosing to act without a plan amounts to placing one's destiny in the hands of random events and that is a difficult path to success, whatever the objective. With or without a well-defined goal, charging off into the future expecting to arrive somewhere you would like to be is haphazard at best, and is the basic interpretation here. Purposeful opportunities are practically invisible when one has no idea of what they are expecting to find.

The next step is frustration followed by a total loss of patience. Here one has encountered obstacles that were not anticipated and attempted to push through them. The perceived solution was to push harder. While in the stages of preparation, any good plan includes a realistic assessment of one's limitations as well. There is validity in the words *you can do anything you put your mind to*; however, that carries the most weight as a motivational tool, and it can allow one to overcome, implausible, and even improbable, but not impossible.

More often than not it is the attitude and approach that defines the likelihood of success, and while confidence and desire are each an important aspect of attitude they are not the defining ingredients. It can sometimes take very little to transform confidence into stubbornness and egotistical behavior, and as a result the approach will be adversely affected. As for desire, it is both the initiating factor and the propulsion, but it is not the navigator of the path.

The most problematic element here is not so easily defined in a single word. When one views others as only a help or hindrance to their own objectives, with total disregard for the goals and desires of the others, then disagreements and conflicts are a certainty.

The obstacles one encounters on their path are often intersections with the paths of others. Just like the obvious driving metaphor, a failure to yield the right away and bulling through an intersection may on occasion allow for the appearance of progress, but it will inevitably lead to setbacks and even tragic outcomes. There is no such thing as the more important dream as each and every one of us is entitled to the importance of our own. When you stretch entitlement too far, you are looking at the root of this card reversed.

Three of Wands

UPRIGHT

Accomplishment will come in various stages as one pursues their goals, and the realization that consistent attention to the process is the greatest influence toward the desired outcome. Evaluating the plan and making adjustments where necessary is the message here. As may have been noticed, overseeing the situation is the common metaphor applied in the imagery for this card, and as well, therein lies the meaning of it. Being passionate about an idea is to believe in it and bring it to life by design through a plan that is both firm and flexible.

One must have the ability to see past a previous success and realize the future will not rely on what has come before. The passion described by the Wands is the element of desire that drives one toward their goal, however, the focus of the goal, the end result, should only be part of the point of emphasis. Allowing the passion to evolve into stubbornness and a rigid approach is losing sight of the fact that how one accomplishes something is not the objective. There is no consideration for inappropriate choices here, only reasonable alternatives and adjustments. Being passionate and driven about something does not define as uncompromising or uncooperative.

What was once success does not guarantee future accomplishment, and the opinions and considerations of others has to play an important role going forward. To do otherwise is to be arrogant and inflexible, and that is not depicted here.

Looking forward with limited dependency on past events is likely to be the best response to this card when it appears in a reading. When the pride of past results clouds thinking about the future, the possibilities of success diminish accordingly.

If one were to recall that when they first began their previous successful endeavor, they did not look back at all—there was no existing backward point of reference—then the limited value of what one had already done would surely be clearer. There are lessons in past failures and accomplishments, but they are not defined in absolutes. What sets this card apart is not so much what one has done, but what one is willing to do in the future.

REVERSED

When interpreting a reversed card one will often discover a failure by someone to understand the significance of the message in the upright interpretation of the same card. From that we can easily see here the arrogance and overconfidence that the upright description warns one to avoid. The crux here is not failure, or one's inability to succeed, it is the attitude and approach one is taking, which in turn increases the potential of failure.

We are all likely aware of people who only find glory in success if it was achieved entirely by their own direction and control. These people will choose failure, if they are faced with giving credit to others, so they can exclaim in the aftermath that the plan would have worked if only the others had listened to them. The mindset is that there is no such thing as credit in success; success is credit.

As feelings of pride can replace feelings of low self-esteem, so too can arrogance replace pride in passionate people and situations. The momentum of emotional stimulation is not something that can be left unchecked and be allowed its own path. Using the analogy of climbing, the higher one rises through success, the greater the likelihood of falling with great speed into ego-driven behavior will increase. Of course this is person and personality dependent, but that in fact is the actual point. When does the *I* in the statement "I want to succeed" become the only part that really matters to the goal?

Prior success is not always a prerequisite to overconfidence and arrogant behavior. Feelings of low self-esteem can lead to a defensive mechanism of overcompensation, which also can personify as arrogance and conceit.

As one can see, the common denominator is self-worth. Whether it is artificially enhanced as compensation or fueled by pride and self-adulation, they may very well be indistinguishable, and both describe a difficult road to consistent success. Furthermore, the line between appropriate and inappropriate action may disappear entirely, with deceit, misrepresentation, and much worse, becoming standard tactics when one is driven by ego. There is often no end to what a person will do when their pride in themselves is how they view success.

Four of Wands

UPRIGHT

This is easily identifiable as a reason to celebrate or the celebration itself. A common interpretation is that one needs to savor the moments of victory achieved along one's path. It should not be so narrowly construed to mean that one should just bring others together to honor the one's accomplishment, but instead a sharing of credit to all those who played a role in the success. Expanding further, this event could very well have no exclusivity to it at all and be an open celebration that extends beyond a need to be recognized. Nonetheless, these are possibilities, and big or small, one should take the time to enjoy the company of others with food and drink, laughter, and the pleasures of social interaction in celebration.

    I have always had the personal perspective, based on a likely quite familiar traditional portrayal of this card, where the party appears in the distance, that this card serves as an invitation to attend to one who is possibly reluctant. That speaks of an element where one may believe with so much work to be done, there just is not time for such things. Hard work and diligence are highly commendable, but what of the enjoyment of the journey. The strength of the desire to succeed and perhaps feelings of obligation and responsibility can possibly be overwhelmingly serious, which in turn may adversely affect one's attitude. This of course sheds light on the need for balance in one's life, where priorities are not abandoned but one's enjoyment of life is not absent from the list.

As much as this might be an invitation of sorts, it is no less than an insistence that one should remember to enjoy life and there is no time like the present to plan or participate. One should not take any stipulations from the appearance of this card on who, what, or where, whether it is family, friends, or any combination of all the people in one's life, and likewise, it may be intimate or extravagant, whatever suits one the best.

In my initial assertion I mentioned celebrating achievement, and that should be broadly interpreted as well. In the unlikely event one finds themselves searching for a good reason, I invite you to celebrate the little things.

REVERSED

There are some cards where the interpretation is extremely context dependent because the possible elements to consider are more diverse. This card reversed falls into this category, but it is not a matter of understanding complexity, just an awareness of the situation. To begin with, the possibility that one might be losing ground on their priority list, perhaps enjoying life a little too much may appear here. That is of course a relative aspect to consider, but it should serve as notice to honestly evaluate the current situation.

To pursue goals with any hope of succeeding one must apply balance to their life. Adding another element to this situation, one may be riding a euphoric feeling brought about by a previous success. With the last statement making a nice segue into another aspect, consider that one may have arrived at the erroneous belief that having a previous success will guarantee the next one, and they can spend their time as they please.

It is also a good idea to look at the distribution of credit in a previous success as a factor in the interpretation. Accepting credit and taking credit are far different things and the current situation may be the result of the latter. Many things can change within the perception of one who has achieved an initial success, and the primary consideration is the before and after of the behavior. The hard work and effort of an unknown individual may evolve into an entirely different approach when recognition begins to enter the picture. This moves us in a slightly different direction, where another element to consider is the one who was deprived of credit, whether real or perceived and is now what would be described as disgruntled. The underlying premise still remains in the before and after sense, but this is a demand for recognition, as opposed to basking in the glow of the accolades.

Like the upright interpretation of this card a celebration has taken place, or soon will, but enjoying the moment has or will change the one represented, and not in a positive way. An important thing to remember is that a change is taking place in someone. Previously there was drive and ambition and it has now been lost or misdirected, and the future will be different than one has envisioned.

Five of Wands

UPRIGHT

An appropriate release of aggression is an element that should be considered when this card appears. This can refer to negative energy used in a productive manner or the positive effects of fair and healthy competition. The portrayals of conflicts that are of a life and death nature are mostly just dramatic imagery, but that does not mean that the stakes might not be high in some regard.

Some people are able to deal with stress, frustration, and aggravation, better than others, but the key to this is often an outlet that releases the energy in a way that is not harmful. The message in this card should be interpreted as a reference to challenges in the overall picture, and they can be external and physical, or internal and mental.

Focusing on the need to redirect frustration, there are not any specific guidelines to consider, but the one certainty is that it will at the very least, be counterproductive to keep pushing in the direction that it came from. If one is already frustrated, then that should be a significant indicator that the current effort needs to be rethought. Negative energy can be stored for limited periods of time allowing one to choose alternatives to conflict as a means to release it, but it usually does not dissipate if ignored, and is known to find its own release and take control of one's action with detrimental results.

As a general rule, people really do not like it when things stand in their way, especially if the obstacle is obstinate, and eventually mere inconveniences will become overwhelming if aggravation is left to find its own way out. The need to survive as a species built into us a very aggressive and competitive nature that at one time caused us to fight each other for food and shelter to survive. It certainly succeeded in getting us through our difficult periods in the wilderness, but we no longer have use for it in today's world, and yet it remains within us.

One could argue that we do still need it, and that scientific advancements come from aggressive competition. However, since we have formed societies with laws based on moral and humane standards, it is only those implemented laws, and the enforcement of them, that keep human behavior at acceptable levels in today's world. My point is that our progress as a species, and on an individual level, requires us to release our aggressions appropriately, not just because they are there.

REVERSED

A great place to start when this card is found reversed is confrontational and argumentative behavior. Conflicts arise from differing opinions, obviously, but what of situations that have one stubbornly fighting for an opinion that has, or can be proven to be false. This has to arise from the human characteristics of aggression and competition having more responsibility than just physical survival.

What is happening in these situations is that the same instinct used for survival is protecting one's self esteem, and at times approaching the level of life and death. The concept of actually being right is overwhelmed by the need to win and be perceived as right. Arguments are not about winning, they are about truth, or getting as close to it as possible. Some arguments have a philosophical foundation to them, and others may be as simple as who is in control of a situation or circumstance. That translates into controlling the other people involved and a need to feel superior. The best interpretation here is the why of the conflict, and the real value of what one might expect to gain.

Within the very essence of civility is the realization that one does not have to prove themselves right, and that sentiment is not based on whether one actually is or not. There are occasions when it is important for others to have the correct information, but one still cannot get through to them. In instances such as this, the message in this card reversed is avoiding frustration and accepting futility.

Viewed as an obstacle to progress, this could reflect either side of the conflict where a confrontation that should have never happened in the first place has escalated. Someone will have to relent. Another possible element to consider that may connect to what I have described, but can also standalone, is misdirected aggression, frustration, and even anger. Someone does or says something one does not like and another person in another situation gets the brunt of the aggravation.

As well this may represent a perpetual behavior where one has become the outlet of everything that has gone against the preferences of another. This is characterized by repeated verbal assaults, with intentionally hurtful words, or worse, physical abuse.

Six of Wands

UPRIGHT

One should have that winning feeling right about now or at least a sense of victory on the horizon. The interpretation of this card is based on accomplishment through inspired effort, and a significant obstacle has, or soon will be overcome. There are many possibilities to consider here, such as recognition and reward, and that can be anything from personal gratification to notoriety and financial gain. What constitutes success always has a relative aspect to it, and the only real constant is that one has actively participated in the achievement.

In a no less significant but more simplified form this could be a successful marriage proposal or a job promotion. Beyond that, imagine anything else one could possibly make a substantial effort to accomplish. In the navigation of one's path there will be numerous identifiable benchmarks of progress as well as obstacles to overcome, and the efficacious moments, whether small or large, are what to look for when this card appears. One can expect a sense of pride to be attached, leading to greater self-confidence, and possibly an even stronger effort going forward. Another aspect to consider in alignment with the suit of Wands is that this moment of success and achievement is something for which one feels great passion.

Responsibilities of leadership could expand the implications well beyond the one, as this can represent an accomplishment where someone in a position of authority has led others toward an outcome from which many can benefit. This should lead to a shared happiness by any and all people involved, and the returns for the one should be spread generously among all the deserving. Unrestrained pride leading to arrogance and selfishness over credit is the pitfall here and although not the actual direct interpretation it must be considered in viewing one's attitude going forward.

This is quite possibly a situation where one is entitled to be proud and their efforts should be rewarded in kind, and yet this should also be a card of self-evaluation and awareness as their will be more achievements to realize and obstacles to overcome. Who will assist one and stand by their side when deprived of any credit? One should enjoy the moment of course, but one should be generous and humble as well.

REVERSED

Here one has taken the victory in accomplishment and allowed it to go to their head. This is a representation of credit grabbing and arrogance, the pitfall as I described in the upright interpretation. One might find ulterior motives, selfishness, and self-aggrandizing behaviors displayed in this situation. Promises of shared credit and statements of the nature *we are all in this together* have hidden one's true intent to self promote and achieve upon the toils of others.

Among the other elements to consider are plagiarized ideas and illusions of effort put forth as grand accomplishments. The elements I am describing may appear in hindsight as a betrayal in victory comes to light, or they may depict signs of such a circumstance currently in progress.

As an artist and writer I work alone, yet even so, if there is any value to my completed works, I am hardly entirely responsible. There are people, both living and passed on, that inspire me, influence me, and in many more ways than I can describe assist me in making what one sees in my work possible. I describe this to point out that there is no such thing as an individual accomplishment, at any level, and in any situation. Any perception of sole responsibility in achievement is a fallacy, and this card reversed represents a situation where one believes otherwise.

There are always circumstances where one can greedily accept every ounce of credit for a success without any obvious short to anyone else, but that is still reflective of arrogance, and that leads to another aspect here: lack of humility. One's feelings of individual self worth inflated by pride are always found at the heart of this representation. It is not to say one should entirely dismiss credit – that is their choice – but credit is due where credit belongs, equally shared. In other words, credit is something that can be freely given away to others, but never taken from them.

It is possible to see failure or defeat in the appearance of this card reversed, but the basis of hubris and arrogant stubbornness will still apply. This of course can lead to the inverse of my previous statement, in that blame should always be taken from another, and never given. The mindset that this card reversed defines prideful, egotistical, and self-aggrandizing actions, whether leading to success or failure, should be the primary consideration.

Seven of Wands

UPRIGHT

To what extent should one stand by their beliefs? Do our beliefs serve us, or do we serve the belief? It seems simple enough under most circumstances, but when faced with fierce opposition do we sacrifice ourselves, or sacrifice that for which we have proclaimed we stand.

There are always limits of endurance when in extreme situations, and there is no fault to be found when valid doubts arise or futility is obvious. It is foolish to think that there is only one way to view a situation, and that all will be in agreement with what one has attested as right or the best course of action. The interpretation of this card is the strength of conviction. Whether it is out of nobility, loyalty, or security, it is a willingness to stand firm in one's actions and words. It is not crucial that the belief is right with absolute certainty, as many differences can be philosophical or theoretical without proof to confirm or dispute. However, if a right and wrong have been defined by humane, moral, and ethical standard, and one has aligned themselves within, then this is the right side, obviously.

Defending someone's honor and standing by the thoughts and opinions of those you care about are also elements to be considered when this card appears. If one professes a commitment and loyalty to someone their actions must match their words, even if there are not any witnesses or consequences evident. The strongest way to describe it is that we are never who we say we are, only the person that we prove ourselves to be in our actions.

Who are the most important people in one's life, and what things hold the greatest nonmaterial value to one? Would you sell your integrity for what looks like a better deal? Is there really a choice to be made in the current situation? That is for one to conclude on their own, and in a twist of words this card is reminding one to decide that they do not really have a choice to make. People can be thought of in a positive light for their words, but not for hollow words of intent. To correctly interpret the appearance of this card in a reading one must recognize the challenges that they face, and the significance of how they act in relationship to their words.

REVERSED

The gratification of winning an argument is never paramount regardless of whether one is in fact right or not. The difficulty more often lies in the need to win, not the actual difference of opinion. It would seem foolish to stand firm in what one thinks when there is substantial information to the contrary, but that does not always seem to be the case. How actual facts fit into one's position has to be considered, but that may not be true when this card appears reversed.

Irrational arguments against credible knowledge can represent one element here, but in the instances where philosophical differences are propelling the disagreement the need to win is also visible. Winning an argument is not the same thing as standing firm on one's beliefs. The inclination to enlighten the misinformed is a common experience I am sure many of us have had at one time or another. When confronted with stubbornness, it can sometimes be difficult to let go, and what you end up with is an escalating argument full of recriminations that will likely veer off into angry insults.

An individual with low self-esteem and/or wounded pride may never concede, and there are plenty of situations where it is futile to even try to persuade them. There is a bit of a dilemma when interpreting this card reversed, since it usually takes two or more people to make up the situation it describes. This card reversed can conceivably be in reference to either or both sides of an argument. It can take enormous strength to walk away knowing one is right without having to win in the face of an irrational challenge.

Does one actually have to win an argument to be right, or continue to be right in the aftermath? Furthermore, does winning an argument make you right when you are in fact wrong? Neither of these are true, and that is the most important element to take away from this card when it is reversed. That is the primary representation, but another aspect may apply in its place. The unwillingness to be true to your beliefs, or act in loyalty toward those you care about is another possibility.

An aversion to conflict is not necessarily a bad trait to have, but there are situations where words of intent may have been used and never meant. Selling one's beliefs and loyalties to the highest bidder to serve their own pride or personal gratification is not a good choice to make.

Eight of Wands

UPRIGHT

Communicating with each other is probably the most significant of all our abilities, and in this era, it can be nearly instantaneous. The process of inquiring and responding is not defined by time duration, as waiting is waiting. Whether waiting for a response from someone or expecting a delivery, there is often a sense of anticipation.

What is primarily described here is that one has initiated a process and is awaiting the results. When finding this card in a reading, it can be an indication that a response is imminent, but that is not a certainty without the context. Further expanding the possibilities, the interpretation can refer to several variables, like an actual visit by someone, or hearing from an old friend who has not been central to one's life for a while. If one hears seemingly *out of the blue* from someone, there was an initial process in some way, perhaps as simple as having provided the necessary information for contacting someone, even if one never expected that they would hear from them.

There are always several processes of communication in motion, and the interpretation of this card is not contingent on the communication being at the forefront of the current situation. If one is waiting for a response from an inquiry, the positive or negative of the message is not depicted here; it can go either way. Anticipating an answer and in turn receiving that answer stand completely isolated from whether or not it will be what one wants or expects; that determination must be found elsewhere.

Tarot readings can easily become overcomplicated if one is looking for a certain answer. One might be well advised to apply *Occam's razor* to their interpretations, and see the cards in the reading without the subjectivity of expectation and hope. That door can swing both ways with trepidation and fear on the other side.

This card is quite benign in its meaning, and to properly interpret it, one must only expect to hear from an entity, receive and object, or be visited by someone – nothing more is stated here. The included element that a process is in motion is an aspect that only serves to enhance one's ability to relate the meaning to their current situation. One final thing to consider when this card appears is a call to patience if one is struggling with their anticipation.

REVERSED

The temptation here might be to view this as a harbinger of bad news, but the more specific interpretation of this card reversed is that the current level of communication is not productive, and perhaps much worse.

The meaning of this card when reversed lends itself well to the digital data transfer age as protracted battles of words rage daily between anonymous sources. Communicating dislike and disapproval is a strong element here and the ability to do so without revealing oneself allows people to express negative feelings quite freely. The interpretation here does not automatically include unknown identities in any way; it only makes the behavior more prevalent. Focusing on nonproductive and negative communication is the key.

Moving deeper into behaviors that might cause this card to appear in a reading, you might find impatience or unrealistic demands. A conflict arising over how quickly an answer could or should be provided is a possibility, as well as what one can and cannot do for another. Personal perceptions of importance and the desire for instant gratification can and will alter expectations severely, bringing harsh and crass expressions into lines of communication resulting in an escalation of ill will. It comes down to a matter of approach, and acceptance of circumstances, or in other words patience and understanding. Once a malevolent approach begins it seldom ends well, even if the resolution seems satisfactory. That one must relent leaves one a victor and the other a victim.

Aside from the direct conflict described, there is also the possibility that an internal conflict is taking place within a single individual who finds themselves waiting for a response. Torn between hope and pessimistic expectations, one can become fixated upon a result, where every moment of thought reverts to the *when* and *what* of the situation. Thinking something bad will arrive and knowing something bad is forthcoming can feel the same to the individual.

Positive thinking toward the moment is not the solution, but to be optimistic toward the ability to overcome in the aftermath of an unwanted response will make a difference. To embrace a potential negative response does not mean that one must accept that all will be ruined, instead it provides an opportunity to prepare alternative courses of action.

Nine of Wands

UPRIGHT

A card that portrays a defensive readiness and a diligent awareness is the common description, although some elements may push a little harder toward insecurity and paranoia. Has one been charged with the responsibility of guarding against a possible onslaught, or has one taken it upon themselves, based on a belief that it might be possible? There is no doubt that being prepared for realistic events and awareness of when they may occur are prudent behaviors, and that may very well be the case here. One can look to the previously described Eight of Wands, where one is living in the anticipation of bad news, and readying themselves defensively, as a possible element to consider when interpreting this card.

It has been said that worry is what you do before you act, and one might want to consider whether their preparation is actually worry in disguise. Evaluating possible outcomes and thinking there is bad news coming, or an imminent threat, is fairly common behavior, but at some point there should be a distinction made between what one *thinks* will happen and what one *expects* to happen. Thinking is often just imagination that has run off in a negative direction, while expecting should require some form of tangible evidence to support that something bad will happen.

This does not include the mindset that *bad things always happen to me*; unrelated negative thinking from precedent does not count. It is entirely possible that one is just prepared for the next in a long line of bad things they think will keep happening. One could throw either insecurity or paranoia at that last statement and they both would stick.

The interpretation of this card stands at being prepared and operating a defensive position for an impending event. The elements of real or imagined go to the context of the situation, and that must be considered for this card's presence in a reading to have a useful meaning.

Looking deeper, how much does it take for one to slip into mistrust, a symptom of paranoia, even if their initial need for preparation was valid? As one contemplates this card, they should not see it as confirmation of their behavior, either way, but instead, an indication that it would be best to evaluate their thinking and expectations.

REVERSED

Getting caught off guard and being unprepared when it does matter is one possibility represented here. Another possibility for the interpretation of this card when found reversed is taking a situation too seriously. This will lead to intense mistrust and suspicions, which is sure to damage relationships. If one has initiated this line of thinking they are sure not to believe another's denial anyway, as paranoia feeds itself, and must be abandoned, not proven one way or the other. If one is currently in a situation where things really are not as they seem, and someone involved does have an ulterior motive, a confrontation will not make any difference. The other involved may not confess, and become defensive, leaving one still being described as paranoid and distrusting, even if they are right, and it is not likely to lead to a positive resolution.

The interpretation here can lean toward not looking closely enough at a situation, and that would leave one unprepared, but there are certainly circumstances where no matter how diligent one is, they still might not see something coming. If that were to be the case, then the appearance of this card reversed should certainly serve as notice for one to be prepared in the situation.

Being caught off guard, or being surprised, does not always refer to a bad outcome, but invariably that is how the event will be perceived here. Being blindsided by someone or something often carries a negative connotation by the simple nature of being caught unaware. It is highly unlikely this refers to a surprise birthday party or the like, unless one just absolutely hates them. It is primarily a representation of something that is unwanted. Since the reverse of this card describes events unknown, it may also expand to cover obstacles on one's path that one did not expect to encounter.

Among the elements to consider aside from the aforementioned are the intentions of the other person or persons involved. The ripple effect of others upon one's path does not make for intentional sabotage, but then it is still a possibility. Being aggressively distrusting and suspicious will not improve the situation and may result in making an outcome far worse than it would have been otherwise.

If one trusts another, it is extremely likely that it is with good reason, and to abandon that due to a possibility represented only by the presence of this card reversed is missing the point. I cannot emphasize enough the need for understanding context.

Ten of Wands

UPRIGHT

It is easy to view this card as a good old-fashioned work ethic, yet there is so much more here than what is on the surface. Escaping into mind-alternating substances is not the only way one can hide from other less comfortable elements of their lives; one can hide in hard work as well. Overall, transferring grief, despair, or any other negative force into productive energy is a good thing, but it cannot serve as a permanent shield; the negative situation will seep through, and possibly bringing with it more negative forces like resentment. The primary interpretation of this card is excessive work, and aside from the aforementioned escapism, other possibilities include oppression, or feelings of indispensability.

Once one has taken on the weight of responsibility, a feeling of great burden can follow, and what was at a time tolerable, perhaps acceptable, has now robbed them of their ability to enjoy other indulgences. This again can lead to resentment of others, as the burden seems to grow with each passing day.

One can come to believe that they are the only one giving effort, or the only one that is capable of making a difference. There may very well be truth to both of those possibilities, but the emotional affect is the necessary point to take from the interpretation of this card in a reading. One cannot simply abandon their responsibility, especially if there are others who depend on them, nor should they embrace self-sacrifice if there are reasonable alternatives available. If one has come to question the circumstances, then this card has made its point, but it does not provide a solution, only how they have come to view the current situation and their resulting feelings.

Outside pressure associated with demands and expectations of a career or job, financial setbacks, or debt, are likely candidates, but those possibilities are not limitations. It is obvious to state that one is not happy about something in their life, and are either working too hard to hide from it, or they feel they are having to overburden themselves to provide.

One more thing to consider here is that it is not just a situation that is difficult, it may be leading up to becoming intolerable without change, a threshold soon crossed, and decisions made when one has had enough, are often quite rashly made.

REVERSED

When this card is found reversed it is a positive reference to productivity and usefulness, where one is able to balance the responsibilities in one's life with taking time to relax and enjoy other interests. In effect, this is releasing one's burdens, whether they are of an emotional nature or a solution to the demands that have been placed upon them.

There isn't any quit revealed here, only that alternatives to what once drove one to the brink of total intolerance have been realized and implemented. This is also specifically not to say that one has only accepted their situation and chosen to deal with it, but rather the weight has actually been removed by decisions that have brought about a change in the circumstances.

If one has been using work effort to hide from other areas of their life that they did not wish to deal with, they should have now faced and overcome them. Negative things that stick inside of us can be avoided but they must be addressed to move on from them, even if they are not immediately purged. As I previously described, acceptance of a situation does not work here; coming to terms with something only offers a temporary solution at best. Whatever the responsibility or demand upon one is, it is there for a reason, and at some point they chose it as part of their path, or made a decision that led up to the current situation. Assuming the path has not changed dramatically, the various aspects will have to come to coexist. The presence of this card reversed indicates they have, can, or will.

Although I sometimes describe the interpretation of a card in a singular point of reference, as for example the present, their value can be effected by what position they fall into in a reading. One must make the determination by its position of whether it did occur, is occurring now, or soon will occur. I will not belabor that point as long as one promises to keep it in mind. In looking forward with this card reversed it indicates that there is a solution or alternative that can make a difference, but one must recognize them and make the change.

One further consideration regarding this card in general, is what of those people that truly do enjoy their work, and really do not mind long hours. I ask them to explore the feelings of those who they invited or brought into their lives—they are also important.

Ace of Cups

UPRIGHT

The first stirrings of positive emotions, perhaps love, are described here. The greatest of all things we feel often have small beginnings, and the interpretation of this card is that beginning. There are opportunities all around us but there first must be an internal interest to spark a feeling before we can see them. The basis of what we enjoy is nurtured in us as we grow and develop who we are, and yet there are still many people or things we find ourselves drawn toward without understanding the reason.

When we experience the first moments of realization it can seem like a mystery to us, but the temptation persists, and we tend to seek it out, sometimes in longing. Following a path to an appropriate love or desire is a birthright, and the important question is, will we pursue in the direction of our feelings. Our feelings will identify it when it is near and guide us along the correct path, and the appearance of this card can tell us that it is close. When one is in their youth, these feelings are new and may be confusing, yet even so, the emotions will gain strength and guide them toward someone or something of emotional value. In other cases, when one is older something may seem lost and forgotten, and although more familiar, they will also be drawn toward someone or something through the strength of their feelings.

All of the Aces represent beginnings involving the elements of their respective suits, and as for the Cups it may very well be of a romantic nature, but it is not limited in that way. There is also the water aspect of the suit of Cups to consider, and it can represent consciousness, or awareness, on many different matters. If that were to be the case, the emotions would continue to be the guide to follow. Where this comes together is in one's feelings, which is how we tend to depict our emotions on a situational basis.

By being consciously aware of our feelings, what feels right and wrong about someone or something will be clearer. In truth, we are not limited by our emotions, we are divined by them. The ability to experience such powerful feelings is a blessing, and on matters of love and romance there are no other feelings that can compare.

REVERSED

Here we find a tainted beginning as something within one is not as it should be or seems. As one's feelings begin to stir there is something that they are feeling that does not fit the situation. Internally this could emanate from past experiences or possibly unrealistic expectations. The difference between something felt and something expected actually lies only within the expectations.

We often see exactly what we expect we will see as we enter into a situation. The comparable behaviors one has seen before are much more powerful when one is watching for them, and of course after the first alleged recognition, expectations will lean further toward the negative and trigger conflicts as one attempts to avoid repeating a mistake. It seems simple in words to distinguish between real and imagined, but when strong emotions driven by love are part of the situation, perceptions and reality can get blurred quite easily, fostering denial.

One must be aware that the door can swing both ways in the interpretation of this card reversed. Aside from resisting when being drawn in through emotions it is also possible to acquiesce, in the thralls of love, when one should not, with both leading to a possible unsatisfactory or even tragic outcome. The expression *falling in love* is a pretty accurate assessment of what happens when feelings of love begin to stir, and to fall is to admit one is not in control.

There is yet another possibility found in this card reversed, and that is unrequited love. This can range from open rejection to an illusionary reciprocation that is unfulfilling, and also can be hidden by denial. Just as I earlier stated that it is possible to see negatives that do not exist, so too is one able to be influenced by imaginary positives. My primary focus here has been romantic love and although it is not an absolute in interpreting this card, it should be obvious to what this card is referring.

An understanding of one's own feelings before examining a relationship or potential relationship is far more than prudent, it is a difference maker. Accepting that a situation or relationship is not going to provide the fulfillment one seeks is not easy, but is walking away from a real opportunity any better?

Two of Cups

UPRIGHT

Even though this card has the ability to be interpreted in broader partnership strokes, I prefer to focus on the strength of the romantic element it portrays. The suit of Cups is representative of emotions and there is nothing more significant than the power of love. Here we have a foundation of substantial attraction that when explored can lead to feelings of chemistry and destiny. There is no greater feeling of partnership than what one experiences when they feel they were meant to be with the person that drives these feelings.

Certain aspects such as love, devotion, loyalty, and harmony are all found in this card, and not in any diminished sense. Its presence may mark a beginning or a replenishment of a relationship, but it does not offer you a choice. A partnership in love will happen. Love as a two-way flow of positive energy does not present decisions unless there are cracks somewhere, and this card does not describe a situation where proceeding might be a mistake. The one possible exception to the *all is well* interpretation might be presented as a reminder for one to realize that they already are in the relationship of their destiny.

The mutual feelings that two people feel for each other often grow so strong that they seem to be able to sense what each other is thinking at any given moment. There is an appreciation that encompasses all five senses and influences their feelings of love toward the other in the most positive of ways. That is what this card represents, but you do not need this card to tell you that; you surely already know when it exists in your life, or I think that you would. With that sentiment in mind the heart of this card is expectations about the future. As is always the case, the value of the question you ask before a reading is vital to what this card can tell you. It allows this card its best potential to reawaken something that is being taken for granted, or perhaps to make you aware that someone you seek is looking for you also, and you are on the path to finding each other.

Expanding on the all-important question, if you do not ask about love or romance the interpretation of this card can expand to other significant relationships in your life. There can be other two party relationships that feel right and have great meaning in one's life, and there are no limitations on how many people are involved as this could represent any mutually beneficial partnership when expanded.

REVERSED

Here is where we find the cracks in a relationship, and even though there are a myriad of possibilities, the interpretation of this card reversed really is not very complicated. Seeds of doubt and unfounded mistrust are difficult to overcome in a relationship as they can linger, sometimes underneath, while other times overtly causing conflict. For me to depict that unfounded suspicions are equal to acts of infidelity would be unfair; however, the end result can easily be just as bad.

Destroying a relationship in jealous anticipation of an event never confirmed is obviously not a productive way to express love.

There are other cards that can express betrayal or deceit, so one must consider why this card reversed appears in one's reading.

As the upright version of this card can represent the beginning of a relationship, the reversed has the strong potential to represent the end. Although not intended to mean insignificant, it can be that simple. The reason may be something that has matured over time, leading to a seemingly trivial catalyst for the break up. Another element that should be considered in this situation is one partner taking the other for granted and/or failing to meet the emotional needs of the other. The brighter the fire burns in the beginning the easier it is to notice when it dims.

Open communication in a relationship is a wonderful ideal, though the word *receptive* is probably a better choice than *open* in that statement. If properly applied it may have an effect if this is found as an outcome card.

The so far unspoken aspect of this card is how it applies if one is currently not in a relationship, or partnership. There isn't always a direct connection, as the person for whom the reading is for might be in a position to feel the ripple effects that result from the disillusionment of a separate partnership that they are not involved in, and this has the potential to alter the perception of whether this is a negative or a positive.

There is always a possible paradox found in the cards when doing a reading; something that might be described as a self-fulfilling prophecy. To alleviate this possibility, do not look at the appearance of this card reversed as evidence to create or confirm suspicions, as proceeding under unfounded beliefs may very well be what is being represented here.

Three of Cups

UPRIGHT

The interpretation of this card is often broadened to include aspects that I believe lose sight of the significant bond that women share, and it is my opinion that those broadened aspects can be found elsewhere in a Tarot deck. Proceeding in that light, to celebrate what it means to be a woman is something I can never fully understand, but that does not mean that I cannot recognize it around me. The abundance that is the Earth, the giving of life as the harvest, is the abundance of the woman. That is the bond that weaves them together, and the many is the one, and the one is the many. This concept is often far out of reach for a man. To celebrate as women together in this bond is the element of this card that contains the primary interpretation.

Women uniting in celebration of newfound love or the impending birth of a child are possibilities that one might consider. They may be reasons or opportunities, but at the heart of it, they are not the underlying purpose. Whether they are sisters, mother and daughter, school friends or work friends, they often come together because they feel close, and enjoy each other's company.

The suit of Cups is associated with emotions and the most powerful of all are the ups and downs of love. Great strength is needed to transit the sometimes-tumultuous waters of romantic love, and that strength can be found in the consistency of love found in true friendship and support that the bond I have described here provides. Now having said all that, one must always take into account the person the reading is for in order to arrive at the best possible interpretation. If it were to be a male with the question, then looking to a mother, sister, or female friend for support might be a possibility. There also might be the potential need to emulate the strength of this bond in one's relationship for the purposes of support.

However, returning to my original contention, the most likely meaning is a need for the man with the question to understand and accept such a bond between women when one of the women is his romantic partner. This implies that the man may be jealous and feel threatened by the situation, or that there is a feeling that a disproportionate amount of time is being spent with her sisters or friends.

REVERSED

The reverse interpretation of this card is the natural flipside of the relationships women share with each other, where bitterness and long held grudges are the focus. At my own peril I would like to point out that just as women are able to maintain strong bonds and long-lasting friendships with each other, so to can they harbor feeling of ill will toward each other for extended periods of time. At additional risk to myself I might also mention that a competitive nature and rivalless behavior are not exclusive to men. To that end, this card represents a dispute or strife between women, but not absolutely defined as either short lived or of long duration. That determination is defined within the context of the situation. As is the case with all disagreements and disputes an amicable resolution comes from locating and addressing the source, not by treating the symptoms.

There are several elements to consider when interpreting this card when it is reversed in a reading, and among them is the nature of the bond between the women involved. In relationships involving parents or siblings, what may appear to be a crisis of major proportions may in truth be minor, and the result of graduating feelings of frustration.

A historical perspective between two people can work either way, both in overcoming or escalating. The difference can be found in the presence of malicious intent, which is certain to lead to escalation. Personality clashes can usually be resolved in compromise and adaptation, and are often more easily overcome.

This need not be limited to families as friendships can be as strong, but the family environment has the additional aspect that the people involved may have a frequent need to interact regardless of how they feel about each other. If that is the case a need for reconciliation is paramount since animosity does not tend to just linger, it grows at every encounter until it is resolved.

Beyond the disagreements and conflicts between two people who have every reason to overcome it are situations that are much darker. Looking farther into the possibilities we can find destructive envy and an obsessive need for retribution. Women do not exhibit these behaviors exclusively, but as I previously mentioned, I believe the focus of this card is relationships between women, and that is what I am describing.

Four of Cups

UPRIGHT

Fulfillment is one of those things that we pursue with the understanding that we will know it when it has been realized. In the inverse do we know it when we once had it and it is now lost to us? Apathy is a common descriptor for the interpretation of this card, and with good reason, it fits, but only to a point. By definition, apathy makes no direct reference to what one once felt, and now no longer feels.

The interpretation of this card refers to a loss of interest, or that one is no longer excited by situations that once held great interest. Since the suit of Cups refers to emotions, then one can rightfully connect love to the situation, whether it involves an activity or a person. As I will often mention, expectations and perceptions play an important role in how one feels about a situation and this card is certainly no exception. This makes an obvious case for disillusionment, where an ideal becomes a rigid standard that has no hope of ever being met, and nothing is ever going to be good enough.

One can make the case, and I often do, that there is no absolute reality, only our various individual perceptions. With this in mind, consider what the difference might be between what one has convinced themselves to expect, and how they see the various current aspects of their life. That is a simple matter of perception, and if the person or activity that once excited one has not changed, then one's perception must have. The point here is to look first at yourself before you lose more than just your interest.

This card is not about the end of relationships or situations, but it can certainly lead up to that if one is taking another for granted or does not come to fully understand what is affecting them. People will change and that is most evident in their perceptions, and those come from expectations that are then compared to the current situation.

There is a built-in human paradox that one may or may not choose to believe, but it is inherently true. It exists as motivation, drives ambition, and is the difference maker in our successes. What it amounts to is that happiness and fulfillment are found in the pursuit of happiness and fulfillment. The nature of the quest, built upon our dreams and desires, must be fulfilling to drive us toward our destiny. Waiting for a future event to provide happiness is depriving oneself of a fulfilling life.

REVERSED

A good way to relate to the meaning of this card when found reversed is to remember what it feels like after recovering from a cold or the flu. A reawakening after a time when things seemed bland and one's energy felt depleted. It is not a new feeling one feels after the effects of illness wear off, but by comparison one often feels more alive than they remember from before they were ill. One may even want to consider my example as an actual possibility when interpreting this card as renewed spirit and revitalization being at the heart of the meaning one should apply. Reversed meanings can often represent a bookend to one having experienced the situation described in the upright interpretation, and that may be the case here.

One will find renewed interest in relationships and events, and one's feelings will be more confidently expressed. There is certain to be a catalyst, but even if new elements are introduced externally the renewed feelings are brought about by an internal transformation. And on the other side, since fear of loss is ultimately a more powerful influence than the desire for gain, then one might certainly consider that as the possible turning point as well. Envisioning one's life without an entity deemed important may snap one out of it, so to speak.

One should be able to determine that there is often suddenness, if not an epiphany to what this reversed card describes. If it appears to be a gradual reawakening there is still a point in time where it began. With Cups being the suit of emotions one can expect that their feelings for someone or something has been affected in a positive way. Lethargy and boredom are elements that have dissipated and awareness and appreciation have returned. With renewed awareness new opportunities will be noticed and attended to in appropriate fashion.

Taking it to the fringe of possibilities, one might consider a change of heart on emotionally related matters, such as romantic relationships. When considering this possibility there are certain areas of a relationship, of which I will not be specific, where needs may not have been previously met, and a new approach or experimentation has reignited dwindling passion. And that is all I have to say about that.

Five of Cups

UPRIGHT

The quite familiar expression often spoken in an environment of tragedy and pain is that *we all grieve in our own way, and in our own time*. This is undoubtedly true, but the interpretation of this card refers to one getting lost in it, and unwilling to move on and take comfort and hope from the blessings that remain. There is no possible way that one can impose a timeline on another, and well meaning relatives and friends notwithstanding, one just has to navigate this path in their own way. In that regard, this can be a difficult card to accept because it can speak of things one may have already heard and pushed aside. I would consider the meaning of this card to be encouragement above anything else, for the very reason that pain endured and overcome is a personal matter to consider.

Quite often, artists use imagery that depicts the tragedy of physical death as the catalytic event, and I am not an exception, but what is described here is not actually limited in that way. The end of a relationship is another powerful weight that can fall on one as well. The internal, if not verbally expressed, feelings of *what am I going to do now?* can ring around inside one's head for extended periods of time. Sleepless nights and lethargic days become consumed by thoughts of what once was, in a mind that cannot be distracted.

Feelings one once expressed, or wish they had expressed, can now feel trapped inside with no place to go. Dreams are filled with those now gone, for whatever reason they left, and there is an emptiness that stretches from here to eternity. Others cannot tell one when to let go, or even how, no matter how much they care. The significance of any card in a reading is a personal message for the one with the question, and any situation that brings about the appearance of this card deserves that same respect.

The love and sincere support of the others that remain will light the path to a better outlook in time, but not through offerings of unsolicited advice and guidance. It is the willingness to sit with them in silence, if that is what one wants.

REVERSED

Sooner or later we all find our way back from the tragedies that life throws at us, and this card reversed can describe that return. Getting on with one's life in the wake of emotionally traumatic events is difficult, but never impossible, even if it seems that way. Here one has a newfound appreciation for whom and what remains in one's life, one's blessings if you like. Most of one's thoughts and memories are now pleasant and the future seems hopeful and promising again. There are remnants that may bring sadness on occasion, but they are no longer overwhelming. Coming to accept and adjust with a desire to go forward marks the elements here and that is found only within oneself. Others may have been supportive and helped along the way, but one always moves on when they are ready.

There could be someone new in one's life, or perhaps someone from the past, and the role they play is an important element to consider. This is a card of time; time needed, time taken, and the time to move on in life. Also described here are gratitude and appreciation for the opportunities one has had, and those that will come in the future.

There is a possible lesson learned depending on the situation, and one should now be ready with new solutions for troubling events of the past. The interpretation of this card when reversed does not always describe that happiness has been restored; it also can point to a willingness to start looking for it again. One should consider the desire to let go of events of the past as the primary aspect to consider. Whatever the nature of the tragic mountain one has just climbed it was never insurmountable, and when this card appears reversed, it should get easier as one proceeds.

One of the best aspects of this card reversed is its ability to reinforce positive feelings about the future and confirm one's feelings that they are ready and able to explore that future, and find new happiness in life.

Expanding the interpretation here one could be contemplating a lost relationship, and coming to the realization that they had only been comfortable in the familiar and that the situation is actually better this way. What was once considered a great loss has now come to be viewed as the right choice, even if it was hard to make or accept.

Six of Cups

UPRIGHT

Everybody should be able to find a cuddly warm spot somewhere in their memory, and it can be great fun to explore. The smallest trigger can open up a gateway, and it can be activated by any one of our senses. Once activated by a nostalgic key, our visual memory comes to life and that is what is represented by the presence of this card in a reading. People, places, and events all come flooding back at the sound of an old song or a familiar aroma. However, this card should go much deeper than a memory when an old lover reappears or one goes home to a place they have not been in a long time. One should not come to believe that this represents a sit-back-and-wait approach; perhaps one should send a message or plan a trip.

Bringing someone or something from the past into one's future can be a positive influence and make life more enjoyable, and this should not be confused with dwelling on what once was, or regret over paths not taken. This card is expressing more than nostalgia, as memories of the past and dreams of the future both live only in the mind unless one takes action. It is not out of the question that someone from the past will contact you, but I would not make that assumption.

What one takes away from this card, just as all others, comes down to their own situation and perceptions, and perhaps one has already been reliving certain memories; thinking of old friends. That would certainly seem to make the appearance of this card a call to action.

Another element that might be represented here are the feelings associated with one's children, or those who may be in the family or familiar: watching them grow up, sometimes happy and proud, sometimes sad that they can't stay young forever. One sees them every day and watches them closely, yet one day they are older, and a difference is obvious, as if you had not seen them in years.

There is one more possibility that one might consider with this card, and that is a sense of playfulness and fun that may be subdued by responsibility and the demands of adult life. Perhaps here is an assertion that although there are times to be serious, one should find time to be as a child, and carefree at times.

REVERSED

Has one come to believe that the past is really better than the present, or is it that the events of the past do not have uncertain outcomes? We all have an innate fear of the unknown and it might seem better to face a known bad ending of a situation than one that lingers in doubt. An element that must be considered is that something has changed; something was lost, and if it was love, it might seem irreplaceable. The interpretation of this card is primarily one's failure to let go of someone or something in the past, and move on in life.

It could also be that one has refused to grow up and become a responsible adult. Although similar to the aspect of not letting go of the past, not growing up will leave one much less likely to function in adult society. It might be described as a lack of maturity, and one might not even be consciously aware that the choices they are making do not meet the standards expected of an adult.

Sometimes people will fail to adjust to the future as it comes along, and sometimes people will become wholly disillusioned by it, choosing to live their life without any forward progress at all, as if time will stand still for them. Sadly it will not, and promising futures are left unclaimed, while destinies are left unfulfilled. Everything will become a memory in time, no matter how hard one resists, and making new memories to occasionally relive is part of the path of life.

This card reversed can also describe that someone is about to open the closet door and reveal one's skeletons. Something in the past, either forgotten or feared is, yes, about to come back and haunt one. I wouldn't say that everybody has dark secrets, but it is likely there are things that many people would prefer were left in the past. This card both upright and reversed refers to one's past and what role it will play in the current situation, and it is possible with the proper approach to turn something negative into a positive. Be aware that the reverse is also possible.

Seven of Cups

UPRIGHT

Dreams, we all have them, and they can range from the grand, to simple differences we would like to see in our lives. Whatever the dreams are, they represent an ideal of a life we wish to live. Our mental capability to envision them also allows us the ability to realize them and enjoy them in a virtual sense, rewriting events and outcomes that always leave us with a happy ending to any situation.

With this ability comes the drawback of comparison to the real world where others can affect events and outcomes less to our liking. There is also the convenience of attainment without diligence and effort to consider. The interpretation of this card speaks directly to the matter of choices made in one's life by comparison and convenience as life relates to their dreams.

One of the elements to consider is an inability or unwillingness to see anything but the desired outcome without regard to the path one must travel to make it a realization. That would speak to a matter of convenience, but also might be reflective of one spending too much time enjoying the dream instead of planning their approach.

What also might apply when this card appears is escapism, as any situation one finds themselves living in likely has perceived room for improvement. One should remember that everyone has a dream, even those who appear to have everything they could want in their lives still live a greater ideal within their mind. It is human nature to imagine more or better in life; thus, all considerations are relative to the individual. If such dreams, or daydreams by distinction, could be truly prophetic, showing one what the future will be like for them, then one might someday see themselves sitting and staring off, living their desired dream in their mind for eternity.

Dreams are important to us and they often bring comfort and hope, but they do not by their existence alone come to fruition. To understand this card is to see the difference between what one wants the outcome to be, and what will happen without real world action and effort. Of course this is a clearly obvious concept to grasp, but this card appears with a message for someone to dream less and act more, and that brings to light the possibility of unrealistic dreams that can only exist in the mind, and some might consider that escapism.

REVERSED

There are several elements one might consider here and realizing the difference between idle dreaming and one's dream being obtainable is a great place to start. There should not be any emphasis placed on how grand the dream is as long as it is realistic. The path to a desired outcome, what might constitute a dream becoming clear is a possibility, and is directly connected to one's ability to determine that they can make their dream come true. When one envisions a traversable path to their dream, they have placed the dream in the distance and connected it to where they currently are in life, in the real world. To do this is a result of clear thinking on the matter, and clarity about what is real and realistic, is another element of this card when found reversed.

What one puts into a dream and what one takes out of a dream are often dynamic elements that can represent what one expects to find when the outcome is realized. There isn't any perfection in the world per se, but there is the individual idealization of what one wants, and that can represent something just as difficult to obtain as perfection. If one wants to participate in a protracted quest for the *exactly what I want* dream, it is likely to be a never-ending journey. Knowing that one will need to be flexible in the dream is an aspect of defining the path.

Another significant aspect here is the desire to decide, and perhaps best described by, knowing the path is not actually choosing the path. Elements of determination and resilience to realize the dream are important to consider as well when interpreting this card reversed. It has been said that anything worth having is not easily obtainable, but that should not be a deterrent to trying. In this situation, that has been faced, accepted and expected to be overcome.

One should not see success as the final outcome here, but failure is also not revealed here. What is found here is that one understands how to make their dreams a reality, and is willing and determined to do what it takes to make them come true.

Eight of Cups

UPRIGHT

There are various possibilities of why, but the primary element in this card is walking away from a situation. Following the emotional association to the Suit of Cups it could very well be a romantic relationship that has lost something, and no longer feels as it had in the past. Two people who have come together to form a relationship still travel two paths, or they should. The first thing one might consider is whether the two paths are still compatible. Just as the common likes and dislikes of two people define their compatibility, so too should their plans for the future. Sometimes lost in the initial surge of love, that feeling of chemistry or destiny, are the futures of two separate dreams. I am not meaning to sound unromantic, but the heart starts what the mind must adjust to in the future.

Adjustments and compromises by both individuals are necessary aspects of sustaining a relationship and that leads us to another element: inflexibility. In reference to my previous statement one would be mistaken in the belief that when two people join romantically there is now only one path. A single path is the result of a sacrifice by one of the two and even if it initially arises in knowing and willingness, it may very well eventually lead to feelings of entitlement on one side and resentment on the other. It should not be too hard to guess which one is likely to walk away if the situation is not addressed and resolved. When there is inflexibility on the part of the one whose path was determined to be of greater importance, whether agreed upon or not initially, the outcome is predictable.

The appearance of this card may also describe where two paths have been maintained, but have now diverged. I will not say people can change, I will state that they will, either subtly, gradually, or dramatically, and two individuals growing and developing together does not easily happen on its own. Another possibility is one or both is taking the other for granted, which can be devastating to a relationship, leading to feelings of inadequacy or disillusionment.

One should also not automatically assume that the one walking away is justified or even making the right choice in leaving. That certainty is not depicted here. And as well there are no absolutes on what type of situation is being abandoned. Specifics are found in awareness and understanding the context of the situation.

REVERSED

When someone chooses to end a relationship or situation, there was a decision made by them to move on, but not necessarily an acceptance. As well, the other person involved may not agree with the decision and has also not accepted the move. This card reversed can represent the acceptance on the part of either person involved. This differentiates from the upright interpretation since coming to the realization that something should end and walking away, is not the same as acceptance. There is always a transitional period of adjustment.

One can walk away from a relationship and struggle with the choice afterwards. When one has a substantial emotional investment in a relationship there is an evolution, or devolution, of feelings that must take place to reach acceptance. The level of how much one still cares in the aftermath is relative to the individual and never specifically defined, but one should always remember that the opposite of love is not hate, but indifference, or neutrality if one prefers. That brings to light that acceptance has not occurred until all peaks of emotion, including hate and anger have dissipated.

Depending on how tumultuous the end is, and the relationship for that matter, one can see why there is a difference between realization and acceptance. The lingering effects do not have to be negative as one could cling to the love that once lived, possibly classifying it as unrequited love.

The interpretation of this card when reversed can be the bookend to the moment or event described by the upright interpretation. To extract the best possible meaning from this card reversed, one might choose to focus on the relatable feelings, whether it applies to oneself or another.

There is also another element here that should be brought out, and that is acceptance does have the potential to swing the other way. It is entirely context dependent, but as I stated in the upright description the decision to move on is not certain to be justified or the correct choice which allows for a possible change of heart when this card appears reversed. Accepting the situation is at the heart of the interpretation here, and one may come to accept that it was/is in fact a good relationship.

Nine of Cups

UPRIGHT

We may not always acknowledge our wishes as such, but we all have something that we would like to come true in our lives. The interpretation here is that it will be realized. There are two aspects that often stand out about the concept of wishing for something, with the first being one seems to be putting the outcome in to the hands of others, and perhaps one feels as if they themselves cannot effect the situation. The second aspect that is noticeable about wishes is one's awareness of them being granted and then taking full credit for the outcome because they made the wish.

Whether one is wishing for an opportunity for love, success, or the resolution to a situation, the key aspect here is that one will know it as their wish, or deepest desire when it is realized. The elements can be quite diverse since each occurrence of this card is going to mean something different to each individual who it appears for in a reading. One may consider satisfaction and fulfillment in life as overall possibilities, as well as financial security and successful achievement. In addition, I certainly would not want to exclude love and romance from the possibilities.

An important thing to remember is this represents a finite point in time and that a granted wish does not come with a lifetime guarantee. If one takes something for granted, such as being provided with an opportunity, which is all anyone can really wish for, remember that what arrives, can leave, as others will have their own wishes as well. Situations involving other people are always symbiotic.

All in all, this is an extremely positive card and can represent anything one might imagine within the limits of possibility. What can really make the presence of this card unique is when one's wish describes an outcome that does not directly affect them. Making a wish that will benefit others is a great wish to make and although there are several cards that can represent the realization of a personal desire, this card stands alone when one has focused their wish on the benefit of others.

Generosity of good fortune is not relegated to only after the fact, and this, in my opinion, is the best possible interpretation of this card one can make. Since wishes are abundant in nature, the results can and should be shared before they are realized.

REVERSED
When reversed, this card often refers to just what I described in the upright interpretation, where someone has taken an opportunity for granted and the outcome will be bleak. In reference to relationships, appreciating someone in our lives is to remember that they do have a choice and one should never allow them to find reason to feel regret. Any situation is at risk if one loses sight of how important opportunities can be in their life, and this is not limited to personal relationships.

There are those who do not think in terms of gratitude and appreciation in any form, but the most likely element to consider here is forgetting. Many opportunities can present themselves if one has nurtured the idea, and their positive outward effort will it a reality. Here that has been lost by complacency.

Elements to consider might include self-gratifying behavior and overindulgence in various unproductive or destructive activities. The usual two-way flow of energy found in a healthy relationship or situation is now moving in one direction and the satisfaction of the one is now the perceived purpose.

I feel it is important to bring the concept of destiny into this description because it has the ability to be misunderstood and lead to self-serving behaviors. If one has come to see a relationship as the fulfillment of destiny, then a misguided belief that once done, it cannot be undone, may generate a complete lack of concern for consequences; they may come to believe that there aren't any. Two people fulfill the destiny of each other, and it does not work any other way.

With the primary aspect of something lost or slipping away intact, any number of behaviors such as neglect, unfaithfulness, self-indulgence, and even abuse can play a role here. Irresponsible money management could apply to a relationship or another type of situation, as can many of the other possibilities, so the focus should not be narrow in the interpretation of this card reversed.

One might notice a before and after in the behavior, whether previously hidden or a transformation, as what once mattered to someone is no longer a priority. When all things are considered, this does not represent an ending to a relationship or situation; it is the reason why something did not, or does not, change.

Ten of Cups

UPRIGHT

If one is looking for a storybook ending, they have found it when this card appears. Of the entire group of positive outcome cards, the Ten of Cups places more emphasis on the infinite possibilities of love than any of the others. The bond of family loyalty and love is the fabric of our lives.

The interpretation of this card is very straightforward, and refers to people who genuinely love and care for each other as a family. There are exceptions, I suppose, but I think most of us want a life filled with the unconditional love found in children, and an understanding and supportive spouse. Those two elements are the definitive meaning of this card, and one does not have to look much deeper to understand the appearance of it.

There are feelings of comfort and security that just happen when the family is together, and we all know what makes a house a home. Such a situation should not be diminished by idealization, a sort of romanticized family that once existed in one's hopes and dreams, and is now presented as a comparison. That and taking the situation for granted are the two primary pitfalls of this card. One should embrace and appreciate who they have in their life, more so than what they have acquired in a material sense. This card can expand across intertwined families, often referred to as in-laws, special friends, even pets, and other familiars. There really are not any limits involving living entities.

The cards can represent a future event, a possible outcome, or serve as a reminder to look around and be aware in the current situation. Some elements to notice are devotion, loyalty, and compassion. All of which are frequently associated with the situation that is represented here.

Another aspect that defines this card is sacrifice, and this does not mean one should give until it hurts, but instead, I am describing that one should show gratitude for the choices others might have made. It is one thing to accept someone else's sacrifice, but it is entirely different thing to expect it or take it for granted. In a situation where positive energy radiates outward from each one to all the others in the group, you have a family, and there is no greater feeling one can have.

REVERSED

Picking up right where I left off in describing the upright interpretation, here we have one or more people taking in the positive energy being given, and either not returning it or giving off negative energy to the others instead. It will not work, and it will not last; one can only give so much without getting anything back in return.

Those who demand sacrifice from others usually accompany it with a challenge of proof that sounds like *if you love me, you will do this for me*, and that is nothing but pure manipulation. The cracks one might find in a family environment are often exploited as an advantage, and the situation will quickly become adversarial. There is no such thing as a loving family environment when there is an, *everybody for themselves* mentality.

A family is a separate entity, the aggregate of its members, and should be thought of as having its own needs. The house and the utilities provided are tangible examples of this, and harmony and compromise represent two intangible elements. A problem with the structure can affect everyone living in it, as can selfishness and disruptive behavior. One cannot expect that everyone will always agree or that there won't be conflicts of interest, but finding a solution that fulfills one's wants or needs without demanding involuntary sacrifice on the others is addressing the family's needs.

Relationships begin because something is right within it, and they do not end because they are wrong now. They end because what was right is no longer there. One could look at this card reversed as the ending of a family environment, but it will only come as a surprise if one has been living by the motto *what elephant?* The appearance of this card reversed as a representation of a severance would be, oh, I don't know, making it obvious for the oblivious perhaps. My point is that family relationships do not, as a general rule, experience a single fatal blow that came without warning. They end because of discord and strife, a lack of compromise, selfishness, perhaps relentless domination, and this is an assault with multiple impacts upon the harmony of the family complement. The interpretation of this card is not telling one it is time to pack, its purpose is to make one aware that the situation is spinning out of control, and needs to be addressed.

Ace of Pentacles

UPRIGHT

Here is a need to be practical and focus on the foundation of the overall dream. Without taking one's eyes off what one wants, look to the individual steps and how they form the path. Need I say that one has no hope of taking the last step without ever having found and taken the first step? As obvious as that sounds, it is one possibility for the appearance of this card in a reading.

    This can represent a victory, albeit possibly small, but significant nonetheless, as the door has now been opened. One should be aware by now that Aces are beginnings and Pentacles can represent money, so if you do the math, this is a beginning of something of a financial nature. Well, better said, it can be if one recognizes it as such, and that is the primary interpretation of this card.

    In other aspects, this suit also describes things of nature and the Earth. One can apply this possibility to such things as environmental issues, or perhaps a weekend camping trip. One could look to planting a garden, or combining the two attributes of the suit and opening a flower shop. There are various possibilities along the lines of beginnings and first steps, and when one looks at the situation, one should be able to make the connection.

The need to be in touch with the path as well as the dream is what one should realize, and although doors of opportunity will appear along the way, if one cannot see the value, or even the door itself, it can be lost. The path does not move toward one, as nothing is given; opportunity must be found and appropriately taken.

It is very hard to navigate a map that does not have any landmarks or benchmarks on it, and when looking at a geographical map as we travel we check our progress along the way with points of reference. This confirms that we are moving in the right direction, and helps us mark our progress, but first we must recognize which road to take just to get started. This road does not come get us from our homes; we must take the initiative and find it, and that requires we know where to look. Yes, enough already with this analogy, but it makes the point. The interpretation of this card is the presence of an opportunity to start something that one sees as a goal or dream, and if they are paying attention, it is time to begin.

REVERSED

This can be as simple as an opportunity missed, or a misappropriate effort toward a goal. Missing an opportunity can mean one was unprepared or hesitant due to potential risk. There are certain to be opportunities along the way, but they are not visible until one is ready to act upon them. Life comes with risk, not a surprise I am sure, and although the pursuit of goals can add positives to life, it also can create even more risks. Accompanying the fear of taking a chance may be complacency born of a comfortable feeling that one is fine with their current state of accomplishment. Since that reflects an answer to a question in the face of opportunity, one should ask, if they are truly okay right now, how they came to notice the opportunity, and face a decision in the first place.

On the flipside of hesitating is rushing in when one should be more cautious. An overly aggressive, and likely not well thought out, approach will often create conflict, leading to more things to deal with than should be necessary. It sometimes doesn't take much to turn an opportunity into an obstacle, and beyond a blockage of the path, it can very well lead to a setback. This can involve one making promises they know they cannot keep, or have no intention of keeping, and other actions of deceit and fraudulent representation.

I have always felt there is a fine line between laziness and efficiency, but there is one glaring distinction. The choice one makes when there is not a legitimate shortcut to be found defines the difference.

When this card appears reversed, it represents the potential for a self-inflicted obstacle, and the interpretation should involve a thoughtful evaluation of the situation. Rash decisions, do this, don't do that, are exactly what this card is warning one to avoid, and if one looks at a Tarot card, and acts or reacts without thought, well, I guess you could say the point was missed.

The presence of opportunities is not what determines one's success; instead, it is how one behaves when they encounter them. It has been said that money changes people, but then lying, cheating, and stealing to get it makes for an interesting comparison. Is one standing in their own way and losing sight of the most basic elements that the suit of Pentacles represents? That of course would be a practical and grounded approach to life and acquirement.

Two of Pentacles

UPRIGHT

Appearances can be deceiving, and that is a strong possibility in this card. Being overwhelmed and looking overwhelmed are not the same, although they may certainly appear that way. To view one as capable when things are going smoothly is fairly easy, but when the situation calls for attention to many different aspects of a situation, how adept one seems might not always be the reality. Adaptability in dynamic circumstances, or the need to be flexible, is the primary interpretation when this card appears in a reading. The suit of Pentacles is representative of finances but it does not place a limitation on the meaning here. It could very well reference meeting commitments and overseeing obligations of a different nature as well.

To draw out two applicable elements, there is a presence of flexibility and sound decision making described here. So as to not allow those two aspects to contradict each other, one must always realize that a decision is only as good as it was when it was made. The appearance of previously unknown information and the ease at which situations can change do not invalidate previous decisions, making them unsound; they simply bring out the need to reevaluate and make a new decision, and that is flexibility.

To some extent we all manage something in our lives, whether it is as simple as what we cook, when we eat, how much sleep we get, work responsibilities, and so on. Thus the application of this card can be somewhat simplistic up to the very complex.

Viewing another person's management of a situation is a perception that can represent only how it looks, not the reality. The overview interpretation of this card is successful effort, or a need to look more closely at what is actually being accomplished. However, as is always the case with all cards, one or some elements may be all that apply, and that discovery lies in the context.

There is one more thing to consider, and although it is not a direct connection, the foundation of the appearance of this card reflects judgment, either of oneself or another. As I stated earlier, appearances can be deceiving, and whether or not what one believes they are seeing is the same as the total reality is something that must be considered.

REVERSED

When interpreting this card reversed, one will see that what was true in the upright meaning is clearly not true here. If one were to choose a single statement to convey what is described here, it would be: things are in disarray. One cannot automatically assume ineptitude, as failure to see the importance and lack of concern overall, are also possibilities that lead to poor management. A single unmade or inappropriately made decision in a management situation, of any nature, can have ripple effects that will disrupt everything eventually.

Preventing a problem is always easier than containing one, and if one began with a lack of concern, they are unlikely to have the mindset to change their approach before it gets out of hand. Drawing a selfish inference from this behavior is often accurate.

Among the elements to consider while determining the meaning of this card when it is reversed in a reading are indecision and procrastination, which may actually relate to each other, with the former leading to the latter. Withholding decisions until all the pertinent information can be gathered is prudent, but here we may be looking at a debilitating fear of making the wrong decision. It is unavoidable here for me to point out the well-worn cliché, *we learn from our mistakes*, but sometimes we simply don't want to make them – some of us more than others.

Recent studies have appeared that imply, and as of now are inconclusive, that procrastination is part of the genetic wiring in some of us. But no matter, if they are going to shut off your electricity, then promptly pay the bill – end of story.

One more thing to strongly consider here is the possibility that even if one is quite adept at managing situations, there is always a point where anyone can become overwhelmed. This possibility can create a paradox, in that if one is really that adept they should have foreseen the possibility and prepared accordingly, thus avoiding the disarray. However, situations are not always consistent in their mechanics, and various circumstances can contain anomalies that by their nature cannot be predicted or prepared for adequately. That leads me to connect the appearance of this card in a reading to my last sentiment, and that is as a warning that an unexpected circumstance or event will be introduced into the current situation, and one might wish to be prepared for an unknown eventuality. Yes, I know that seems incongruous, but it is still true.

Three of Pentacles

UPRIGHT

There is creativity in all of us in some form or another, and to be rewarded or lauded for bringing an artistic vision to life is at the heart of what this card represents. It primarily focuses on one-of-a-kind works, from a child's crayon drawing to what one might find hanging in a museum. Furthermore, there are no limits placed on the medium and it can depict writers, musicians, sculptors, moviemakers, fashion designers, and so forth.

There are several elements, or traits, associated with this card that can be considered as well. Aside from the ability to see or hear things that are not yet a reality, you will find a very detail-oriented nature and extreme patience. One's level of success overall is not a factor, as this can describe recognition as well as reward, and one does not ensure the other.

In my opinion, there are more aspects of the other three suits here than the actual suit of Pentacles of which this card belongs.

There is creative intelligence, a love for what one does, and a great passion or fire in doing it. It's been my experience that artists usually aren't grounded, and many are not driven by material reward. That isn't to say those factors are always true, but an artist who this card would represent in a situation will certainly have a strong association with the elements of the other suits.

Expanding the possibilities you will also find perseverance, and a very high standard. Using the trait aspects of this card it can also describe the completion of complex tasks that aren't necessarily unique in the end, but the method of accomplishing them is revolutionary. The common standard for this card is reward and/or recognition, and that is certainly accurate, but the various elements, aspects, and traits are the keys that unlock the best interpretation in a reading.

I want to make one aware that this card represents a good example of potential ambiguity in a reading. When looking at this card one must recognize things like patience, perseverance, and attention to detail in the event there is no known artistic endeavor for it to describe. To be lauded for unique effort; a higher standard of performance in any one of many different tasks could be the meaning here. There are a number of ways that innovation can apply, and although creativity is the primary focus it shouldn't stand as a limiting factor when interpreting this card.

REVERSED

There are various possibilities when considering why one's efforts are not being put forth, and not the least of which may be that their heart is not in it at all. In determining the difference between what one is expected to accomplish, and the end result, the obvious place to look is not their ability but their desire – the key word being expectation, which sets a standard to be realized and which presumes one's ability. One would wonder why someone would take on a project and not give it their best effort. Whether it is an artistic endeavor or any project with a defined completion, a possible underlying sentiment may be a desire to speak of having done something as opposed to actually doing it, and there is a difference.

There are other elements one might consider when interpreting this card when it is reversed, and one of those is obstinacy. When confronted with the opinions of others or helpful criticism, even from a member of an intended audience or recipient, and devaluing their input, then one presumes only they themselves know best, and that is egotism driving stubbornness.

One may also look at the possibility of deception in the way of fraud or plagiarism when the situation involves an artistic or creative endeavor. This meaning would lend itself to undeserved credit and reward being obtained by someone. As one can see, the interpretation here can be diverse depending on context, but what remains constant is that something of a creative or innovative nature is not as it should be in the end result.

Another aspect that might be considered is to what point the one in question, artist or writer, what have you, may be stuck, and perhaps best described in the familiar term *writer's block*. The element that applies to a creative block is often a narrow focus born of dissatisfaction, the result of seeking the perfect word to write or the perfect color to add. Creative people are naturally detail oriented and as a general rule they do not see any insignificant aspects of their efforts. This can manifest as another type of stubbornness as they seek to precisely express their thoughts or the visions in their head.

Four of Pentacles

UPRIGHT

The acquirement of material possessions can foster greater desire, or greed, and can lead to paranoia. This is the essence of the interpretation of this card. As I have written elsewhere in this text, the fear of loss is greater than the desire for gain, and that will always be true no matter how powerful the desire becomes. It can lead to fear and mistrust, culminating in isolation as a means to protect what one possesses.

As one's greed perpetually fuels their behavior and suspicions consume them, their personal relationships will fail and die. They will view their skeptical behavior as a shield and laud themselves for their mistrust of others as a prudent way to protect themselves from those they believe are acting only out of envy. It is nearly impossible to make someone aware of this unhealthy behavior as they will surely view it as a trick to undermine their ability to protect what they possess. Any two or more people gathering and talking without the one will become conspirators against them, whether or not they are known by the person.

As is always the case, perception trumps reality and irrational acts become justifiable in the mind of someone caught within this downward spiral of obtainment and security. When interpreting this card in a reading, it is commonplace to focus on the effects this type of behavior has on others, but the cause must be considered as well.

We sometimes look at behaviors such as this as some sort of mental deficiency run amok, and that really isn't always the case. Regardless of what one views as the inception of humanity, and all life for that matter, the instinct to survive is undeniable. Collecting, hoarding, and protecting provisions for our individual survival is not really a choice: it is the means to our very existence. In an era where protecting one's food and shelter for survival has escalated into protecting one's way of life, it is still driven by the same instinct that we really aren't that far removed from.

It is not my intention to condone, but to explain what is truly at the heart of this behavior, and in turn what this card represents when it is found in a reading. To understand comes easier when the why is considered as well.

REVERSED

The interpretation of this card reversed is somewhat unusual in that it is not an escalating or aftermath representation. This card is not alone in that sense, but to focus on what we have here, the obtainment of possessions is not driven by greed, and a willingness to share is evident.

To be ambitious by itself is not greed, it is how many of us go about our business. This is only a small part of what is represented here as the primary element is what one does with what they have acquired. You will not find any paranoia in the reversed interpretation of this card, and one's ability to maintain relationships is not threatened or damaged by their actions. They do not isolate themselves in fear and are always willing to listen to and help others if they can.

A person's success does not put limitations on this card. Someone who shares what they have with others qualifies, even if they have barely more than nothing. I did not use the word miserly to describe the upright version, but it certainly can apply there, as the inverse, generosity, is applicable here. The significant aspect to consider with this card both upright and reversed is the mindset of the person to whom it is referring.

In my description of the upright, I wrote about the need to survive being the basis of one's actions that have been redirected in this era. Given that, the door is open here for having developed a different perspective, and whether it is a learned behavior or a Scrooge-like epiphany, the foundation may likely lie with one's ability to overcome an inherent trait of primitive survival.

It is not a good idea to evaluate and share with others a personal point of view that would describe a developmental distinction between people. That is not the point. What it does offer is an understanding that behaviors do not have to be permanent and all the factors that go into how one behaves are both born to us and learned.

How to apply this card reversed when it is found in a reading, as is true with all cards and I have repeatedly pointed out, is based on other factors relative to the one for whom the reading is done. It may be another, you, or a need to emulate the behavior described within the card.

Five of Pentacles

UPRIGHT

Here is one down on their luck, not very happy about it, and holding the more fortunate responsible. Resentment and bitterness radiate here, as life has treated this person unfairly in their mind, and everyone needs to be aware of their condition. It may represent falling all the way into destitution or any situation where conditions have become less than sustainable.

One can feel a sense of rejection and isolation, even hopelessness, but despair is not the reaction. Anger and hate, often with feelings of betrayal by others lead the emotions. They likely brought the situation on themselves or at least had a hand in the circumstances, and it is often perpetuated with an obnoxious need for pity that pushes others further away. The attitude is the key when interpreting this card and the relative nature of the circumstances is not defined, although by association with the suit of Pentacles there might be a connection to one's finances.

There is not anything easy about overcoming difficulties with cash flow, but at the same time it is not hard to make it worse if one wallows in their misfortune and resents others that are in a position to help. It is difficult for me to imagine someone as having nothing but endless misfortune, but without entirely disputing the possibility, it is more likely that one is extending their bad luck with their mindset. It might become more comfortable for one to be right about failure than to be wrong about success, and suffer another disappointment.

Limiting the interpretation here to one having just fallen into a difficult situation does not work, since the cards are not known to state the blatantly obvious, and serve one better as a tool of guidance moving forward. That makes the current circumstances a symptom, and when this card appears, it is for revealing the solution, by pointing toward why things have happened.

Making decisions with a lack of forethought, becoming overwhelmed and suffering from the result are not a matter of bad luck. One has followed a path of choices that were navigated by an improper perspective and mindset, and now there is only misfortune and others to blame. Following the same path that led one to this point is not a good choice, change is needed, and it begins with one's attitude.

REVERSED

One could liken this to a spiritual epiphany, or sudden enlightenment, as one has discovered something different about life. The new perspective may be the result of a tragic event and altered circumstances, where one has come to realize misplaced values as their downfall.

This card reversed represents the beginning of new growth, but it does not necessarily describe a change in the environment. That is in the future as one pulls themselves up from the depths to which they have fallen. Even though the change takes place within one, there is a possible significant external influence, perhaps viewed as an angel of mercy. The representation here is not meant to focus singularly on financial recovery, but one's new outlook should lead them in that direction.

A more prudent approach to how resources are used is an element to consider, and this was preceded by a realization that one does not need as much as they once thought. And yes, the ever present cliché, *money isn't everything* may be a part of the new thought process. There isn't any indication here that one will give up a material-based life and go live off the land in the wilderness, but the change in lifestyle can be dramatic.

As one can see, this card reversed marks an end of an era in one's life, and as I will say time and again, an evaluation of one's perspective and expectations is often at the forefront of progress toward change and greater enlightenment. What goes wrong in one's life will not go away by beating their head against it in anger and frustration.

Overall, the interpretation here does not demand that one has fallen into poverty, having lost everything they once possessed, as the fear of the possibility can bring about introspection and change. Setbacks and potential setbacks will create a fork in the path, and often, choosing which one to take is not a thought-out decision, but a habit in one's behavior. Just like driving on familiar roads or walking through one's living space, where we relegate the navigation to an unconscious mental function, so too can one move through life without conscious awareness of the direction they are taking. This sense of guidance is a pattern of choices we have come to make with such frequency that we go down a certain path because that is the way we always go, and don't stop to wonder if it might be wrong.

Six of Pentacles

UPRIGHT

At first glance, this card is altruism, philanthropy, charity, generosity, and any other word you can think of that is associated with giving to others in need. The spirit of giving of oneself or what one has, for the benefit of others, is certainly the predominate interpretation when this card appears in a reading. However, another aspect that can play an important role here is what or how much the giver gets in return for their generosity. When one gives to another in a one-to-one situation, the giver feels a certain sense of satisfaction of having brightened a moment for somebody in need. This furthers their feelings of self-worth and makes them feel like a good person at heart, and by no means is there anything wrong with that in any way.

Further consider the feeling that one creates internally when giving, and expand it into turning one's charitable donation into a production where the giver is able to experience the adulation of communities, societies, and even the world. That this would serve the giver to such an extreme does not diminish the gift in the slightest bit, but the true spirit of altruism is defined as putting oneself at a disadvantage to assist others. In this case, the charitable act provides an advantage to the giver that may assist them in acquiring even more toward their own goals – hardly a disadvantage.

Let me reiterate that this is not a condemnation of such acts, only an element that I believe applies when one is interpreting this card in a reading. To give to another is a purposeful act that benefits the receiver, and if that benefit is intact, then you cannot find fault with it, whether it provides an advantage or creates a disadvantage to the giver. However, it can be raised to a much higher level with anonymous donations where one does not incur any personal reward or advantage for their gift. This card upright describes giving and does not have to be limited to be correctly interpreted, but it can easily be broadened to the levels of pure altruism if it is possible in the current situation.

If one does something for the benefit of another without telling anyone or taking any credit for it then one has transcended terrestrial expectations of generosity and has truly achieved the highest levels of charity that can possibly be achieved.

REVERSED

With money comes the ability to decide how to use it, and when reversed, this card represents inappropriate and even illegal choices. The ability to gain ground toward a goal can seemingly be bought, or there are those who believe that to be true. Perhaps in the short term it might be possible to perceive progress, but it is inevitable that it will not be sustainable and the end result will be a setback of tragic proportions. Secret transactions such as under the table deals and bribes are some of the interpretations we can find here. From that we can determine that any use of money to buy something that should not be for sale is the basis of this card reversed, and any transaction that is, or must be kept in secret, will identify what this card is describing.

There are times when the greater good might appear to be a reasonable consideration, or thoughts of genuine good intentions form a rationale. The broader vision of this card will not overlook the sentiment that *the ends justify the means*. Any true path to achievement and fulfillment will not be upon the backs of others, regardless of the intended destination, and this should be at all times understood.

If one believes their cause is truly noble and the action they desire to take will actually not bring harm to others, then a moral, ethical, or legal judgment has been made by the one. That judgment rests on the belief that they know better than others, and if that is an indisputable truth, then this card will not appear reversed. Good intentions notwithstanding, a financial provision that defies accepted practices of society, whether based on terrestrial or celestial edict, will likely cause this card to appear in a reading. From the simplest of transactions to the extreme, the complexity of the ramifications cannot be discounted, and is often difficult to fully predetermine.

Free will affords one the ability to proceed regardless, but to initiate a reading and not place one's faith in the answers it provides within the cards is an interesting approach, to say the least. If this card appears reversed in reference to someone else, there are other aspects to consider, the most obvious being how it affects you. It isn't always possible to influence others, but any card that appears in a reading about you, will affect you.

Seven of Pentacles

UPRIGHT

Progress is something that is discovered by observation, and in a clearly obvious statement, you cannot see how you are doing if you do not look at your path. To accomplish something, one must work toward it and this card represents the ability or the need to be patient and aware that some things take time. This can apply to relationships, business endeavors, and any number of situations when one has a vision of the future they seek to realize.

There are of course circumstances where accomplishment has a deadline, and there is always a timetable in some form, but situations where speed of accomplishment is the only thing that matters are extraordinary. In a real crisis, a situation where action is required immediately, it still must be a successful act to make a difference.

A published author, whether moderately successful, or a writer of best sellers will have a complete understanding of the concept found in the interpretation of this card. A completed work does not occur without patience and perseverance, and furthermore, the distance from the seed of the idea to the printing, requires repeated evaluation to navigate. Writers and artists make good examples of what one should take from this card when it appears in a reading, and to apply this to any endeavor would be the first step. To define a goal should also be to define the path to it, and the plan to reach that goal is seldom, if ever, going to remain exactly as it was originally conceived. The necessary adjustments require awareness and honest evaluation.

The suit of Pentacles is associated with money and the material but the strongest elements found in this card, patience and evaluation, are not limited to goals that only include finances. Relationships, romantic and otherwise, also should be developed at a reasonable pace. Is there a difference between looking for the person of one's dreams and looking for someone to play that role in one's life?

When beginning a relationship, what one feels, which may be described as chemistry, can be somewhat idealistic and accelerate the growth. It certainly seems unromantic to not just go with it and enjoy it, but then again the desire to be in a relationship as opposed to developing it gradually with patience is likely to involve perceptions that are altered by expectations.

REVERSED

When people see something they want, it immediately joins them in a dream or fantasy where it has become a part of their lives. Certain things can become real in one's life quickly, such as buying an article of clothing, but larger and more substantial things often require a plan, patience, and perseverance to become a realization. That distinction can be difficult to make by some people at times, and that impatience is the primary element of this card reversed.

A failure to form a plan isn't at issue in this interpretation, as machinations are in fact plans as well; they are just inappropriate shortcuts that will lead to disillusionment and failure. With unrealistic expectations as the starting point, then fed by the misguided belief that having without diligence is the same as earning, one is likely to find themselves unfulfilled.

If one formulates the appropriate plan and soon find they are being thwarted by obstacles the dream may appear in jeopardy. Since they had already mentally taken possession of their goal they are now operating under the fear of loss, which is far greater than the desire for gain.

Anyone who has ever shopped for a new car or other big-ticket item will likely have experienced this first hand. A salesperson will soon refer to the object of your possible desire as your car or your sofa long before they get your money. They will then proceed to tell you why you need to act now, thus giving you the impression you will lose something, as opposed to acquire something. This particular psychological trick can just as easily be played upon oneself, leading to the illusion one must act now or lose out on their dream.

It doesn't take much thinking to see the terrible ramifications of applying this to the beginning of a relationship with someone. The best pace for developing a strong relationship is never faster than the slower of the two involved. If one comes to feel that the other person wants them to push the speed of development, then one really needs to think about why that would be true.

Yes, life is short, but the concept of living every day as if it might be your last, rushing into things just in case, has an adverse affect on the future. I certainly do believe each day should be cherished and enjoyed, but as an all-consuming behavior, it will make the future seem the same as today. One can decide on their own if that is what they want, but rushing into relationships, and other aspects of life, may be, for a lack of a better way to say it, settling due to impatience.

Eight of Pentacles

UPRIGHT

A common one-word description of this card is *craftsmanship*, and that is certainly not in dispute. The ability or the need to concentrate fully upon the task at hand is the leading element described here. From concentration comes diligence and attention to detail, two underlying aspects also represented here. If I might first ask forgiveness of William and those who recognize it: If it were done, when 'tis done, then 'twere well it were done correctly. Yes, I altered it, but writing that was a lot more fun than any other cliché about doing things right I could come up with to make the point of this card. There should be the presence of pride in the workmanship and effort, which translates into caring enough about the results that one's full potential is realized.

Do not assume a direct connection to one's job or career, although it is a possibility; just allow the situation and the desire to find the area of focus. In the end there may be the possibility of financial gain, but even though the suit of Pentacles does have a financial association, not everything is about money, including references made by this card. It could be nature related, but that is also only another possibility, as anything that is better with best effort could very well apply here.

Another element that should not be limited is whether one derives enjoyment from the effort, other than their pride upon completion. Many endeavors could apply here that reflect only responsibility, and are undertaken simply because of their need to be done. In that light, the significance of this card in depicting a dedicated work ethic is revealed, but again, there isn't anything here that says one cannot enjoy the task at hand. One should interpret this card as drawing attention to the value of how one goes about their business, regardless of the actual end result involved.

Although I favor the Three of Pentacles as more likely to depict artistic expression, it certainly could apply here as well, with attention to detail and concentration being essential to artists and a mainstay in this card.

From that reference one could easily include the evolution of ability to make each result better than the last, which would certainly apply to a musician practicing an instrument.

REVERSED

There are various possibilities when this card appears reversed, and they all lead up to defining someone's effort, or lack thereof, toward an endeavor. It is broad enough to include fraudulent results such as plagiarism, as well as laziness and a lack of concern.

One possibility to consider here is that one wants credit for having done something without actually having taken the time to make an effort. Pride like anything else can be stolen or inappropriately acquired. One should find that either deception of effort, or deception of intent are possible, as one may state they will do something without any intention of doing anything. Consider that there are those that will make empty promises to perpetuate situations and relationships, and the promise is the extent of their effort. A lack of desire does not necessarily translate into laziness, as the task may not be important to them, and one is using intent to placate someone, and it is usually followed by excuses and more promises.

As I mentioned, this card reversed may also indicate one is taking the credit, and possibly the reward, from another that has made the actual effort. This may be a onetime act, but it is often a reflection of a behavioral deficiency, perhaps that has been acquired through previous successes with such deceptions.

The primary interpretation here represents the attempts of someone to benefit from accomplishment, whether before or after any action was taken, regardless of whether any was taken at all. Also possible here is halfhearted and careless effort one might describe as shoddy workmanship with at times dangerous implications.

There are times when one might feel a need, or demand, for quantity over quality where choices are made that impact their ability to adequately meet both standards and the former becomes the priority. Even though such a situation may absolve one of responsibility it is still reflected by the meaning of this card reversed.

One may also want to consider that someone has overstated his or her abilities, and of course that is also an effect of pride. All references to pride in this card reversed might be referred to as false pride; I do however prefer undeserved pride instead, as one might be taking pride in their deception.

Nine of Pentacles

UPRIGHT

This card pulls from both the practical and material, or financial associations, of this suit. There is a strong underlying current of financial independence, and the comfort and security it affords. The traditional depiction on this card is of a woman, which I have honored, and is just as important and relevant today as it was in the past. Although I cannot personally relate, I do believe I can understand the significance of a card portraying a woman successful in her own right. There isn't anything provided here; everything is earned, and purely by her mental acuity. Along with her abilities one will find confidence, self-discipline, and practical thinking. One should not limit this to only affluence and should allow for self-sufficiency at any level.

Although in most cases the Court and a few cards from the Major Arcana are the ones chosen to designate specific people in a reading this card as well could carry that distinction. Drawing together the elements of self-reliance, confidence, practicality, ability, and of course a woman, this card certainly can be interpreted as someone in a given situation.

Refocusing on the elements, the most important is a total lack of dependence on anyone other than oneself. That aspect is possible as a standalone representation, and if one were inclined to set aside gender it should be the focus. As for confidence, it has the potential to be seen by others as arrogance, but it is not. Weakness and vulnerability are not found in the self-sustaining, nor are they found in this card. One will see formidability in negotiations, and as well there won't be any allowances for things that appear trivial. Every detail will be scrutinized and nothing is taken lightly. This does not represent someone that it is wise to try to fool or mislead, as this is a thinking person with the ability to recognize situations for what they truly offer, and the overall benefit.

There may be higher education, or at least wisdom from practical experience. One should not expect to see extravagance but there might be luxury and a participation in the arts, as well as society functions. Another identifiable element is generosity toward environmental and animal rights causes.

REVERSED

Look first to a lack of self-discipline when interpreting this card reversed, as squandering an opportunity is a strong possibility. When viewing it from this perspective it is clearly a self-inflicted setback. There may now be dependency as the result of abandoning one's restraint and principles in the euphoria of success or good fortune, where practical thinking is pushed aside and replaced by frivolous behavior and extravagance. Whether one has gone through a sudden transformation or has never done well attempting to manage finances, this card reversed is still pointing toward dependency.

Another area to explore here is corruption such as bad faith deals, bribery, embezzlement, perhaps even extortion. This would describe choosing an alternate and inappropriate path to what one wants. You can pretty much include any level of deceit when applying this element to the interpretation since it describes a mindset that generally has one simple rule; don't get caught. It can range from petty theft to someone who appears to be highly successful.

The elements of inability with finances and corruption are not necessarily mutually exclusive, as it can read as either or both. Clearly this is a situation where someone cannot be trusted, and possibly on multiple levels, involving both their own finances and the resources of others.

There may be extremes of self-indulgence and self-gratification and anyone who can be used will be to no end. They will exploit in the interest of their desires, and the hollow words, *I will make it up to you* are repeatedly spoken. In situations where avarice is present, there will often be promises as well, and in this case opportunities will be presented, but the words are just that, words.

Just about everything a person who might be represented by this card upright does right, the reversed described does wrong. The reversed representation of this card is likely to point toward money, but it should not be a limiting factor in one's interpretation. One can apply these elements in situations that involve academic achievement or competition.

Ten of Pentacles

UPRIGHT

Family traditions do not seem quite as prevalent as they once were decades and centuries ago, but they are still around, and that is the underlying concept behind this card when it appears. Breaking it down into its various elements, such as devotion, loyalty, respect, and pride, will broaden the scope and make it simpler to interpret when it appears in a reading.

There is a difference between devotion and loyalty that can be recognized in a person's behavior. What devotion describes is how one acts in the presence of the person or traditions to which they have pledged this devotion, whereas loyalty is the person's behavior when they are away from them. The same differences can be applied to respect and pride.

As is always the case when interpreting cards in a reading, they are not to be viewed as absolutes in their overall meanings. For example, a single element such as devotion may be the primary message in this card when it appears. Furthermore, the strongest element of this card is traditions of a family nature, but that is not to say that one must follow the career lineage to fulfill what this card describes, but only that they are devoted and loyal to the family as its own entity.

There is no certainty that financial aspects will play a role, but as the suit of Pentacles does bring with it that representation it could very well be possible. What I have yet to mention is the role parental influence may have on their offspring and this card may very well describe a decision on such matters.

If one begins with the family and expands the scope into the various elements included, then the purpose of this card's appearance should be fairly easy to recognize. Different families will of course have various family traditions, but the common word, thus the keyword, is family, and what that means to the person or situation.

There are behaviors and choices that will cause conflict, even strife, within a family, and a detailed description isn't necessary, but the appearance of this card makes the health of the family relationship a part of the situation, and needs to be a consideration in any decisions that are made. Choosing a different path than is expected doesn't have to be an act of blatant rebelliousness, and one's approach can make all the difference in the world.

REVERSED

When one looks at a family from the outside, what they see might be a façade for public display, and the difference within can be minimal or extreme. The nature of family devotion and loyalty can project and/or protect. When this card appears there is something hidden within the family in question, and it may even be contained within a select few of its members. It is possibly a dark family secret, but depending on one's perspective of course, that might be a bit melodramatic. The root of the situation is more likely to be conflict and disagreements that are driving a wedge between members of the family.

Any detrimental behavior, action, or event that can be associated with a society or organization can be found in the condensed society of a family. This can range anywhere from simple disagreements to power struggles and up to much more egregious situations.

What this card reversed is describing might be invisible from outside the family and concealed by denial inside. Among other possibilities that are in the same vein would be past events that have created distance between members of the family, and the lasting effects have a bearing on the current situation. This can be found to manifest in behaviors; the results of emotional or psychological stress or trauma.

Families are expected to, and often do have a lifetime bond and they might frequently find themselves together due to familial matters, whereas two members at odds must face each other because they both care about another member of the family who is not involved in the situation. To fully understand the appearance of this card reversed one must look to the interpretations of other cards in the reading as well as the context of the situation. That is something I have brought up frequently but its importance cannot be overstated.

How familial events of the past, or those yet to come, affect the current circumstances is the primary need of understanding here. The person the reading is for may be outside the family, but is connected to one or more members, and may be involved in a situation they do not clearly understand due to a projected family image. When one is within the family structure in question, it may not be any clearer because it is hidden, or they are in denial.

Court

Page of Swords

UPRIGHT

A youthful vigor and enthusiasm is depicted here, and this is not a person who will wait patiently for events to unfold. This can be the embodiment of rebelliousness, but not generated by spite; instead, by a desire for challenge and participation.

As a representation of an individual, they are intelligent and confident, and they will act out of the belief that they are doing the right thing. Contained by their youthfulness, they will frequently test the boundaries of what they can influence and affect, and they seldom reveal a sense of fear. They can be brutally honest, however, not to intentionally hurt, but because they are of the belief that the truth serves a greater purpose. If they do cause emotional pain they will apologize with sincerity, but will also explain the logic of their words or actions and stand by the value of their choice.

The most common elements here are a youthful restlessness, and a need to understand. Vague responses or descriptions do not satisfy them, and it may appear that their questions are intended to challenge authority, and to some extent that is true, but their goal is to acquire knowledge. This also means discovering the reliability of the source.

Although ambitious, they will be hampered by their impatience at this stage of their life. Not deterred by rejection and resistance they will come back again and again, each time better equipped mentally than the time before. This resilience is another important element to this card, and because of their persistent nature, they will be perceived as being quite stubborn.

The early stages of intellectual development will involve trial and error, and one may see what they believe to be an uncaring attitude in failure, but this is not the reality here. As I mentioned, this represents relentless behavior, and evaluating an error, adjusting, and continuing to move forward are strong elements to consider in this card. What is in the past is not for dwelling, but for learning. What is behind one is a lesson, and the focus of such a person is applying it to what lies ahead, without hesitation.

When interpreted as a Messenger, one will find intellectually stimulating thoughts, ideals, or simply put, things for one to think about, with varying levels of importance.

Of all the elements to consider in this card, this is a situation that requires quick and decisive action, but never without forethought. One must seize an opportunity, or it will be lost.

REVERSED

This could be described as a guided missile without any guidance. There will be the presence of irrational thinking and illogical choices, or at least that is how it will appear to others. As a person, what better serves their wants and needs drives them, and because they are intelligent, they make a formidable enemy, but never a good ally; they simply cannot be trusted.

As a manipulative and controlling personality, they have no boundaries to what they will try, and will move from one approach to another until they are successful at getting what they want. They will quickly learn the pliability and weaknesses of others and will exploit them relentlessly for personal gain. Since they are young their methods will sometimes be obvious, but they have the ability to adapt quickly.

As an obstacle, this may be one's secrets exposed or wielded against them, a situation, perhaps, that does not seem to offer any solutions that afford progress, as at every turn there appears to be no way to overcome and continue. There is no value in attempting to meet it head on, and diplomatic approaches will appear weak, resulting in a strengthening of their resistance.

Overcoming a reversed Sword obstacle requires a legitimate distraction, and that is not to mean subterfuge or sinking to their level. If one is viewed as a threat then a greater threat will distract them, and lowering oneself to their methods will appear as a challenge, much like a game they will refuse to lose. When this card appears reversed in a reading one is facing an intelligent and relentless obstacle. As a person, winning is everything, and everything is a competition.

Other identifying elements here are actions for the enjoyment of negative reactions, and a constant need to disrupt and provoke. Although they will display erratic behavior, one cannot assume they are out of control and are acting without purpose. They will appear subdued, amiable, and even agreeable, at times to gain trust and acquire information they can use at a later time.

When interpreting this card reversed, look at its effect on one's path before drawing all of the elements together to form an individual adversary and fixating on them. If there is such a person in one's situation, are they truly blocking the path or just being enough of a nuisance to be a distraction.

Knight of Swords

UPRIGHT

The representation here is of intelligent and assertive behavior as either the personification of an individual's character traits or, as is common with all Court possibilities, a need to emulate them. Clearly founded on thoughtfulness and just action this card depicts no outwardly expressed fear or reservations at the threshold of action. There are times when bold, aggressive action can appear to be impulsive, but this is a quick and decisive nature that may only give that impression.

There are many facets to this card when it is chosen as a Significator or is determined in a reading that it defines an individual. They often possess great determination and ambition, and in light of that, they are often a person that refuses to take no for an answer, but without applying inappropriate pressure.

Taking action to get what they want and to do the right thing are staples of this card and the person it may represent. They feel that hesitancy, the result of indecisiveness, is fostered in doubt and that is a trait they never display. Even though they are not always right, the prevailing sentiment that they live by is that it is better to act and be wrong than to fail to act due to the inability to decide.

At times the person or personality described here may seem aloof or emotionally distant, yet they will speak in direct terms and hold passionately to their ideals. There is a stubbornness of conviction that is easily recognizable; borne by their ideals and desires to accomplish, they are not a good choice to cross swords with, and to stand in their way can be a risky proposition.

This person is cut from the cloth of leadership and is likely destined to progress into a position of authority with ease. They will establish control over others and situations through the sheer strength of their will. At this stage of life, their ability to be flexible is limited and can be precarious, but they do not act out of the need for control; they assert themselves because they firmly believe that they are right and just in their actions.

Interactions with them will not be slow and methodical; they will be fast paced, intense, and with a quick resolution. The strength of their intelligence will require a thoughtful approach, and they are unlikely to be influenced by emotional appeals. As is true with all members of the Sword Court they can be easily underestimated, and to do so would be a mistake.

REVERSED

The basics of aggressiveness, ambitiousness, stubbornness, and intelligence remain in this card reversed, but throw in arrogance and a need to dominate and you are now likely to have a very volatile situation on your hands. The heart of the matter can lie in the purpose, but the explosive nature of this person or character trait alters the circumstances exponentially.

A master of control they are not without their disarming charm, as it serves to lure the vulnerable into submission. Often prone to strong inflexible opinions their behavior can be heavily influenced by their pride, and specifically any possible damage to their feelings of self-worth. This will manifest as a stubborn unwillingness to consider other's opinions, even in the face of irrefutable logic and proof that contradicts them.

This person will expect to win, feels they are entitled to win, and will use any means they can to win. In this light, they will see every event, including an ordinary conversation as a competition and may apply every tactic including escalating words into a physical confrontation in order to accomplish what they view as a victory.

They will diminish any success by another if they had no hand in it, and will openly insist that others will fail if they are not allowed to participate in the efforts. This seems clear enough to recognize, but an even more obvious behavioral trait that defines them is that they take all the credit while giving others all the blame. As one can see, the potential for tragic results is clearly apparent, but there is yet one more aspect to consider, paranoia. Fueled by low self-esteem, any private conversation, or even the appearance of one, can prompt an aggressive and mistrusting response.

To bring it clearly into focus, the upright interpretation of this card depicts a person who believes in their self-worth and does not act to prove it, but to accomplish. The reversed interpretation of this card describes someone who convinces themselves of their self-worth by attempting to prove it at every turn. The person this card is likely to represent reversed is not without goals or ambitions, or even a substantial level of intelligence in most cases, and that makes interaction with them all the more likely to end in their favor without any consideration of others, because this person will simply not let up.

Queen of Swords

UPRIGHT

In this card, we have an extremely intelligent and highly motivated individual. They are not prone to deceit and subversive actions, but if those who oppose them change the rules, they will gladly accommodate them and act accordingly. Given that they are keenly aware of the people and circumstances that surround them, any attempt to deceive them is both unlikely to succeed and ill advised.

Like the other members of the Sword Court, the tendency to severely underestimate this person is common. Their assertive and outspoken behavior often masks their intelligence and can foster the misguided belief that they can be caught off guard and that they function without structure and purpose. The reality is that nothing could be further from the truth. This card represents a person or character quality that is fair in judgment, but is often perceived to be unsympathetic by those who would invoke their wrath.

When choosing this Queen as a Significator there are certain aspects that can stand out and create a narrow focus. This may limit this card's ability to be correctly interpreted when it is left to appear as it will in a reading. Of all the Court cards appearing in a reading this is the one most likely to be seen as an obstacle or an undesirable outcome when found upright.

They will openly and honestly speak their mind, but not necessarily with cruel intentions. Their ability to think quickly and act decisively leaves the impression that they are impatient and intolerant of others. As I have stated in various ways throughout this text, a person's perceptions and expectations make up their own version of reality. If one approaches a person this card might be depicting with the belief that they are adversarial, stubborn, and difficult, that is precisely what one is apt to find.

Combined with the previously described elements, their ability to exude confidence and authority will command respect and they are frequently viewed as natural-born leaders. An ability to trust others is not absent from their personality, but they will not reveal any weaknesses they may have freely, and will only keep close counsel with a few well-chosen friends. Interacting with a person this card represents may be challenging at times, but they are always loyal to those who are loyal to them.

REVERSED

Not attempting to soften this, I will state that unequivocally this may very well represent a person you really do not want to challenge. The reversed interpretation of this card can depict someone who has only the singular goal of vengeance, even if it takes their lifetime. They cannot be reasoned with, they will not be forgiving, and they simply will not give up.

When this card appears reversed in a reading, the same qualities of the upright description – intelligence, awareness, and decisiveness – are all likely elements to consider, but the motivation is entirely different. A sense of fairness may be expressed, but it is not born of justice, only malicious revenge, their interpretation of fair. The ability to rationalize cruel actions as being deserved is almost always present. One should not assume from this that it describes a person who is out of control and that it would be impossible not to recognize them. They can be charming when they choose and they will use it to bait others into vulnerability to serve their desires.

At the heart of this, one may find unhappiness, disillusionment, damaged pride, or feelings of entitlement. They may or may not direct their negative energy toward only one person, and at various times express that they owe several people what they deserve. What may become evident quickly is their inability, or unwillingness actually, to take responsibility for the failed events in their life, choosing instead to blame others and hold them accountable.

When interpreting this card, one does not have to place limits upon it that speak only of a person with a bad attitude or personal payback on their mind. Other elements such as intolerance or manipulation can be found in situational events that do not require them to be directly connected to the person for which the reading is done. One might find themselves to be an unwitting pawn in the manipulative efforts of unknown others locked in conflict.

As an obstacle, this may be a situation with rules and expectations that can stifle, oppresses, and hold one in fear, affecting them only because they were at the wrong place at the wrong time. What is represented here is the inappropriately applied stigma sometimes associated with this card upright, and when reversed it is certain to represent a point of conflict.

King of Swords

UPRIGHT

Great leaders are often aggressive and stubbornly defiant in their beliefs. Doubt expressed by authority leads to a loss of faith by their followers, and this King represents a person who will instill confidence with the ability to be decisive and committed to their decisions. They possess a strong resolve, and although their self-confidence will border on egotistical behavior, the true nature of their stubbornness is based on the idea, *"do not tell me I am wrong, prove it to me, and then I will listen."*

What emotions they feel seldom reach the surface, and they will express logical determinations on matters of the heart, sometimes making them appear cold. Passionate leadership is one thing, but emotional leadership is an entirely different thing, and not often well received.

An outstanding behavioral element that is described here is that although they do not expect nor plan to fail, they do not fear it, nor wallow in pity if it happens. They will accept it, learn from it, and move on without hesitation. At the same time, they do not act rashly and they are often uncommonly intelligent with the ability to think quickly on their feet. They do not view complete wisdom as obtainable, and will apply solid reasoning with experiences, continually pursuing better decisions.

Other noticeable aspects are a strong sense of justice and objectivity, and they will judge others and their actions fairly and without prejudice. Having said that, they are extremely self disciplined, and are known to project the high expectations they have of themselves upon others.

The suit of Swords is associated with thoughts and intelligence, as well as bold and assertive action. With all deference to the Queen of Swords and even offering her as no less than the equivalent here, this is the apex of authority and respected prescript. All of the Kings and Queens have their positives, but one must consider if they want the same qualities in their lover that they want in their leader. Perhaps one does, but being loving and tender are not strong elements of this card.

This person is often innovative, but not necessarily creative in an artistic sense. They strive to be more efficient and successful in a professional or business sense, which makes them more analytically minded, and this will often be the primary focus of their energies.

REVERSED

This is a representation of a person that is highly aggressive, and that might become apparent quickly. However, they are also often intelligent and disciplined enough to move through situations without revealing themselves in order to get into position to sieze control.

Obvious behaviors they will display are acts of contempt, extreme rage, and unleashing debilitating verbal assaults upon those they profess to love and care about. Expanding on that, their view of love and relationships revolves around the usefulness of others toward satisfying their own wants and needs. Other elements of behavior that apply are possessiveness and objectification of others in relationships, as everything belongs to them and is under their control.

There is not a normal sense of what is fair here and any situation where an agreement is needed they will only compromise if they are forced to make concessions. In such a case they will dwell upon what they perceive to be unfairness and feel they are owed, prompting resentment and disdain toward those involved.

Their warped perceptions of circumstances can turn innocent acts into malicious betrayal and they will relentlessly pursue payback with cold and calculating effort. In that regard, the concept of accidents only applies as an excuse for them. One may also witness a need for attention that does not allow others the ability to pursue their own interests, requiring others to abandon all desires and responsibilities that do not pertain to them.

As an obstacle upon one's path this may represent resistance to even the best-laid plans, perhaps the result of someone who feels they have a greater need for someone else's time. There could be mistrust or a lack of faith that is based on misconceived ideas, or simply used as a reason to keep one under their control. Whether it is directly aimed at one or not, the effects will still block progress.

This would certainly be a person or situation to avoid if one can, but if that is not possible direct challenges will not likely succeed. Although what one is facing will by no means seem to be fair, it is not prudent to act as the obstacle does, and disregard an appropriate approach. Stubborn behavior by authority, real or perceived, will not relent, and one must find a way around.

Page of Wands

UPRIGHT

This is a person with a need for excitement, a lust for life, and potentially a youthful misunderstanding of mortality. As a Significator, they are usually chosen for their youth, and the boldness and daring that accompanies a desire to be stimulated. They can win people over with their charm, and influence them to new experiences with their exuberance.

As a personality type, they have the strong magnetic appeal of an adventurous spirit and those around them can feel their excitement when sharing an experience with them. More conservative minded individuals that witness their behavior often see them as foolish and reckless, but they are driven to feel, and do not sit still very well. This restlessness easily identifies them just as much as their boldness and daring.

This represents a personification of passionate consumption and they will relentlessly drain all the feelings they can get from a situation, as rapidly as they can, and can be stubborn in the face of resistance. This is another sign of their youth as is their potential for mood swings when they explore which passionate approaches bring the desired results. Again, because of their youth, what excited them yesterday may bring about boredom today, but that refers back to their desire to feel an experience until it has been depleted of its ability to stimulate them.

This Page is known to be faithful and loyal to others, but may at times struggle, as new and exciting opportunities enter their life. Further defining their youth: Although they can be extremely creative and artistic, there is a frequent underlying conflict where passion meets patience and the ability to see projects through to completion can become difficult.

This card as a representation of a Messenger in a reading, will bring news that carries a high emotional stake, perhaps involving love, and of course, great passion.

As I will redundantly point out, when choosing this card as someone in your life, either as a Significator or as it appears, do not consider the elements as all-inclusive. For example, Wands are strong willed and at times can overcome their lack of patience. They may also be tempered in their risk taking, as they are quick learners who rarely repeat mistakes.

REVERSED
As a youth, this is a personification of a problem child, or the behaviors one may equate with the label. A lack of restraint is only the beginning of the possibilities found here. There is a need to control and dominate people and situations, using malicious and cruel verbal assaults as well as physical acts to attempt to be in charge. Somewhat different than their thrill-seeking upright counterpart, this is a representation of someone who derives their enjoyment from pushing others outside their comfort zones.

At times they will be stubborn beyond reason and will escalate a situation quickly with their short temper. They can be charming at times, but are prone to severe mood swings, and their shifting demeanor might be described as consistently unpredictable. The elements I describe may seem to make the behavior here obvious, but this person is not always confrontational. They will push the envelope to find the edges, but they are smart enough to pick their battles.

The actual behaviors of a person depicted by a reversed Court card may often be consistent with the upright description, and although at times they do stand out clearly, at other times they can be a precise mimic. They are able to use this to ensnare others and then create relationships where they become a dominating, controlling, authority over them. In the case of this card reversed, and in regards to romantic relationships, this would primarily apply to their charm, passionate allure, and sense of adventure.

As an obstacle, this is a stubborn and seemingly impassable situation, which could result in frustration in the one facing it, clouding the issue and raising the possibility of misdirected solutions. When one encounters an obstacle on their path, the focus should be to find a way around it and continue. What can happen though, is a fixation on the obstacle, not the path it blocks, and that negates progress; playing right into the hands of someone who might be described here.

In the reverse of this card one will often find a perverse desire to draw out the negative passions of others. This offers them the ability to feel justified in their malicious behaviors toward one, and the result is frequently stagnation or setbacks.

Knight of Wands

UPRIGHT
Among the strongest elements of this card are youthful daring and exuberance, and often seemingly suddenly unrestrained. The Knights are often chosen to represent a coming-of-age individual, and here we have a sudden, but not yet totally understood explosion of passionate feelings. Motivated by that very desire to feel, they are quite often known to live for the experience. Although they are bold and speak their mind, they are not crass. By nature, they radiate with confidence, and they will approach an unknown person or situation expecting the encounter to be successful, whatever the objective. They are not easily deterred by failures or setbacks, but they are not really known for keeping their feelings to themselves either.

The perspective of the person represented in this card is still in development and they may move quickly from one situation or relationship to another. They have a tendency to avoid commitment, and if they are faced with one they wish to make it will be made with sincerity, but only if their feelings of passion toward the subject are at a peak.

Because of their effervescent charm, they can be easy to forgive, and in the upright interpretation of this card, they do not intentionally exploit this aspect of their personality. Since other people can feed off of their vitality and enthusiasm, they are often popular and well thought of as a companion. Their positive outlook toward life and endeavors may rub pessimists the wrong way, but it is actually one of their most alluring qualities.

Although artistically talented, they may struggle with patience at times due to their youth. However, having said that, their desire for attention can lead them to such activities as music where the adulation they receive will fuel their fire and hold their interest. They can be as ambitious as they come but what motivates them is found in what they feel, sensation wise, and this will lead them to seek unique opportunities where their abilities will stand out.

When choosing this card as a Significator or interpreting it in a reading it is important to consider how they make others feel about them. As is true for all members of the Wands Court their passions will eventually stand out and influence those around them.

REVERSED

Obsessive and impulsive behavior surrounds this person when this card is interpreted reversed. They pretty much want what they want and they want it now. To the misfortune of those who they become involved with, they do not make good partners. Their view of others is seldom considerate or understanding, and they seek only to possess both objects and people.

They are certain to be jealous when others wander too close to that which they will insist belongs to them. Making matters worse is that they may at times restrain their feelings of having been betrayed, allowing the negative energy to grow until it can no longer be contained, then unleashing it with a relentless verbal assault. Sooner or later everything comes to the surface, and often with a vengeance.

They are not devoid of the ability to charm, and may swing back and forth between positive and negative behavior in an instant. Since they are extremely similar to the upright depiction of this Knight, they can at times be easily forgiven. This brings into focus their ability to deceive and passionately express remorse or evade responsibility for their actions, albeit here it is to further their own desires or reclaim something they have lost.

Their demand for attention will be realized in numerous episodes of high drama as they attempt to garner affection, sympathy, and pity; any attention will serve them. Once they have established a foothold in someone's life, they immediately progress to advanced relationship behavior, and if rebuffed they will not let go easily.

What will become obvious, if it has not already, is that the reversed interpretations of the Court cards have few if any positive qualities. When they appear in readings, they clearly represent obstacles, either in known people or situations where the attributed behavior will have an effect on the current situation. The answer to how one proceeds in such circumstances is best discovered by the person the reading is for, through understanding the situation and the values of the choices.

That such a person who might be represented by any reversed Court card can change may seem implausible, but it is not impossible, and that is particularly true of the younger Knights. How to overcome obstacles is not an absolute science, and all personal considerations are relative to those who are invested in their path.

Queen of Wands

UPRIGHT

This individual or quality may be the most easily recognizable of all the members of the Court. Their flamboyant style of dress, a dramatic entrance, as well as the way they position themselves in an environment will identify them, even in the moments when they are not verbally or physically revealing the true strength of their passions.

When they act and speak, it is with unfaltering confidence and they possess a magnetism that draws others toward them. Often found to be the subject of envy by others they embrace leadership with excitement that is infectious and are natural trendsetters.

The foundation for identifying a member of the Court in a reading or choosing one as a Significator is the level of the behavioral characteristics that can be seen by the observer. There are not always absolutes in consistency of behavior in the Court cards, and using this card as an example, the release of their passions may be only situational. Comparing this Queen to the Queen of Cups will reveal two very loving and passionate individuals, but the Queen of Cups is happy and content within the love, while this Queen will need to make others aware of her loving situation to feel fulfilled.

    Fiery passion is usually considered to be the significant aspect of the suit of Wands, and of course this card represents a personification of that, but more evident here is the reason that lies beneath their behavior. A desire for attention is the source of their energy; the fuel that drives them.

    They are highly likely to be openly flirtatious and tend to see relationships as fluid situations to further their desires. This is not to cast them in a negative light as they can be as loyal and devoted as anyone, but their passions can be insatiable. If the level of what they feel diminishes even slightly, they are not apt to accept it, and they may attempt to reignite the passion, or they move on to recapture what they once had, somewhere else.

    Also known to be ambitious, their ability to conform and follow others can be limited, and they will not sit quietly if they disagree with the ideas and opinions of others. To go unnoticed or have their beliefs dismissed are an equal affront to them, and they will introduce drama, real or imagined, to shift the focus back to them. One can never assume they are pure drama and will do or say anything for attention, as they are often knowledgeable and highly capable problem solvers.

REVERSED
When interpreting reversed cards of the Court you are primarily looking at the elements that make up the strength of the upright description, but now they are corrupt and sometimes even dangerous. This card reversed is certainly no exception, as you will find controlling and egomaniacal behavior that can and likely will be very destructive. The strength of conviction here can manifest as grudges and impenetrably stubborn behavior.

    The desire for attention becomes a demand for attention and will often become apparent in severe mood swings as they use any means they can think of to gain or retain control over others and situations. Like the upright interpretation of this card, it is important for them to share their feelings with others, but here they are spreading their unhappiness.

It is not a common practice, at least that I am aware of, to choose a reversed Court card as a Significator. The question that comes to my mind, especially with this card, is why to do so would be a benefit in a reading. The purpose behind Significators is to connect the querent, you perhaps, to someone specific in relation to events in the past, present, and future. This is usually such a recognizably destructive force it would seem difficult not to be aware of such a person already. The discovery of what role they will play in one's past, present, and future events would be easier to determine, letting the card appear as it might in the reading. This would be particularly true if interaction with a person who has exhibited this behavior is unavoidable, and their reaction to a decision one makes is connected to the question.

There are several aspects of this card reversed that are somewhat less obvious than the aforementioned, such as finding humor in the belittlement of, or at the expense of others. Such a person will likely create a ridged structure of conformity when they are in a position of authority, and offer no leniency under any circumstances when their rules are broken.

They do not accept differing opinions by others as anything less than an attack on their intelligence or authority. Any such situation can escalate quickly into conflicts, and they will not back down, even when they are factually proven to be wrong. As I mentioned previously, they are often easy to recognize and one should be aware of them, but for a time they are able to contain their demeanor until they draw someone in, but eventually, their true behaviors will be revealed.

King of Wands

UPRIGHT

Do not expect to find this person sitting quietly by in any topic of discussion. What they feel, they must share, and they are often intelligent and knowledgeable enough to have a valid opinion on any subject. They thoroughly enjoy a debate and will play devil's advocate to put themselves in a situation. The personification or character trait depicted here can at times be confrontational and challenging to interact with, but they realistically see thoughts and opinions as only having value if they are expressed.

Creative solutions to complex situations are one of their greatest strengths, and they are seldom known to think conventionally. One can also take from that trait an artistic ability apparent in many forms, as they can envision ideas and objects that are not easily conceived by others.

Like the Queen of this suit, this King also enjoys attention and they are often easy to recognize as a result. From a psychological perspective, their desire for attention is only partly motivated by their enjoyment. An equal, if not greater element that influences them is the passionate belief and confidence that they have something important to say and they can make a difference with what they have to offer.

They have just as much a need to experience passionate feelings directed toward them as they express outwardly toward others. If they do not feel intellectually stimulated as well as physically, they will seek it out, but not at the sacrifice of their loyalty and devotion. Although my reference to this element leans toward romantic relationships, there is a prevailing consistency in all aspects of their life.

One of the things you will find me pointing out in describing the members of the Court is that you cannot always include all of the elements to define a card in choosing a person it may represent. Here there is both an authoritative, commanding leader and a passionate artist represented. One works almost exclusively as the center of attention, while the other may be reclusive in their endeavor until its completion, and then garner the attention. Another element that goes hand in hand with this is that passionate leadership is not always patient, and art invariably is slow and methodical. Aside from the obvious, what else this brings to light is that the individual described here is most certainly in control of their behaviors and whether they are being dramatic or accommodating, it was a conscious choice on their part.

REVERSED

It is common in texts such as this one for writers to use adjectives as keywords to describe the interpretations of cards. In deference to those who do and have, I have chosen not to because I seek to further promote practical application. A prime example would be impatience when referring to this card reversed. Impatience is a word used to describe an unwillingness to wait, but here its source has significance. The person this card reversed is describing will be nothing short of arrogant and narcissistic. Expressing their unwillingness to wait reinforces their feelings of greater importance to others, as they see it, and it is impossible to avoid. They will further feed this delusional perception with constant intolerance; being all too eager to pounce on the mistakes of another.

Another behavior likely to be experienced when interacting with such a person is how quickly they will diminish any offered thoughts and ideas that are not their own. They will often proceed to argue against something they know absolutely nothing about. A slightly more subtle aspect of their exhibited behaviors will be that they are the only one allowed to change their mind.

What should become apparent is that there is a constant need to prove something, not necessarily to others, but actually to themselves. The others around them are often merely used as tools to convince themselves of their pseudo superiority. When this card reversed appears in a reading one can anticipate the possibility of confrontation. When we go even further into this personality we will find a demand for attention, and there is not anything more important that cannot be dropped to attend to them.

Do not come to believe that they can be easily identified as they are also prone to charming secrets and information from others to later use against them. Demeaning others for the purpose of dominating them is their signature, and this can often be seen in any, but not necessarily all of the previously described elements.

To view them as this King upright run amok or out of control is likely to lead to underestimating them. The appearance of a passionate individual in itself should not serve as a warning, but the chosen moments of expression should be noticed, and that is the key to understanding the message of this card when reversed.

Page of Cups

UPRIGHT

A good place to start here would be puppy love; that very first crush, when one has no idea why they have these feelings. All they know is that whenever they are around that special person their heart races and they feel strange inside. When they are away from this person they feel a longing, another feeling they do not understand.

As a person this is a youthful heart if not an actual child. They will be innocent but charming none the less. Finding ways to express their feelings they will often write love notes and letters, and even poetry. With a strong imagination, they will be naturally artistic and drawn to music, literature, as well as any other art form that they can use to express their feelings. Often quite affectionate, they are gentle, kind, and eager to please.

They are by nature sensitive and they will fall in love quickly, generously demonstrating their feelings to the one who holds their interest. This is not always a definitive representation of a complete personality type, as we all should be able to recall when we first fell in love. Furthermore, one should not always define this as a romantic type of love as it can refer to feelings directed toward a parent, sibling, or a pet.

Speaking of pets, an affinity for animals will make this person easily identifiable. They will stubbornly desire to bring home and rescue every animal they encounter. Their strong family bond will lead them to actively organize and participate in family gatherings, and although at times they are reserved and introspective, they do enjoy the company.

When considering members of the Court as representatives of the people in one's life the stronger elements are the best guide. Emotional and sensitive people can be intelligent, practical, and passionate as well. It can be difficult at times to see someone in a singular vein of behavior, but defining someone does not have to be complex; the cards will adapt and support your choices. How you see them is how they will appear in your readings once you have identified them.

The traditional choice of using adjectives as keywords to provide starting points can be helpful at times. Words like kind, thoughtful, and caring are associated here, and these elements can stand alone in the interpretation without personifying an actual individual.

REVERSED

A misrepresentation or misapplication of love in a situation is commonly found to be the case when this card is found reversed in a reading. Recognizing narcissistic behaviors in someone would likely be easy, except for the need for a self-loving person to draw others in to get what they want from them. In time the real behavior will clearly show through, but as is always the case with the Court cards reversed, the ability for them to hide within the elements of the upright representation can allow them to get close enough for others to emotionally invest in them.

Behaviors like possessiveness and jealousy will begin to show in their efforts to claim exclusive rights to all the emotional energy one has to offer. In short, as a person, they do not share well. In an adult, this can be childlike games of love where words are spoken with insincerity, and flattery is used as a tool of obtainment.

They are often the first in a relationship to profess their feelings of love toward the other, and the last to let go if the relationship ends. Among the other elements of behavior is a sense of loyalty only to themselves, and will see incidental and insignificant acts by others as great betrayals to them.

When confronted with contradictions in their behaviors they are ready with excuses and will deflect responsibility toward others such as parents and lost loves, anyone but themselves. Their ability to express love even if they do not feel it, can at times make them easy to forgive, but their promises about the future are often hollow.

Every person provides their own perspective on whether people can change, although a more accurate statement here would be *will change*, and I have already stated that I believe that they do. However, when they do, will they become a better person? Someone that might be described here would not be above insisting that they will change for the better to stave off the possible end to a relationship or situation. The sad truth is that they may even speak it with intent in the moment, but over time, when the strength of the threat has dissipated they may revert to their original behavior.

What can be even more perplexing to others is that they may actually care and love another, but they do not understand how actually being in love is practiced to the benefit of both. This can make them genuinely sincere at times, but difficult for others to tell when this is true.

Knight of Cups

UPRIGHT
This card is most commonly representing someone on a quest for love in its simplest interpretation. There are newfound feelings and a need to share and explore them. Their expressions of love are charming and romantic and they speak and act from the heart. Often identifiable by their idealistic approach to situations and boundless optimism, they see good before they see bad in others.

Remembering that they are young and inexperienced, they at times may seem awkward, but they do not tend to be offended when it is pointed out to them. This person can always be found to be kind, caring, and generous toward all life, in all situations. The personification here describes elements of honesty, sincerity, and compassion. Infatuations and crushes are commonly represented here, and as a personification, they are certain to see attraction toward another as something to pursue, and at times relentlessly. In other words, they are not known to be shy about their feelings.

Their open and expressive nature about love will lead others to view them as flirtatious, but they are loyal and take their commitments seriously. One might find themselves under a spell when interacting with someone that is described here, as their powers of ensorcellment can be difficult to resist.

In choosing this card as a Significator, the primary element might be their youth, but their curiosity about the feelings associated with love should expand that consideration into adulthood. Comparing them to the Knight of Wands one will find this person to be softer spoken and their sincerity can be quite captivating. Although less obvious on the surface, they can be equally passionate, and, like the Knight of Wands, they are also motivated by their feelings.

They appreciate a life of refinement and luxury and enjoy sharing it with those they love. Driven by their feelings and a strong imagination, their artistic ability may seem effortless to others, and they have the patience to see projects through to completion.

As an interpretation, this card can represent a time to experience and cherish the subtle aspects of love in one's life, perhaps as memories, or going forward. In either circumstance one should find encouragement and comfort about the future of love in their life.

REVERSED

Deceptive charm and self-gratifying ulterior motives, hidden beneath false sincerity, are two of the most significant elements offered by the message in this card when it is found reversed. Evaluating the intentions and sincerity of someone in the real world can be perplexing. Doubt and suspicion can make a good thing go bad, and yet one would certainly prefer to see the truth before it is too late, and they have found themselves deeply involved in a relationship or situation. Being emotionally swept away by someone often brings with it an overwhelming sense of denial. It can be difficult to distinguish between insignificant flaws and subtle clues of what lies beneath a behavior. The appearance of this card reversed should foster awareness, not suspicion.

Among the most recognizable aspects of a person or behavior described here are emotional immaturity and a clinging, possessive behavior. Utilizing approaches that have successfully ensnared others in the past, they use charm, and offer false promises to move a situation into a commitment stage at a rapid pace.

Also represented here is a situation where one, due to their history, might be vulnerable to such an approach. Among the strengths, if I should dare call it that, of a person this card might describe is an ability to easily detect and recognize those who are susceptible to being deceived by their expressions of love toward them. As well, they are capable of finding the greatest area of weakness in another and manipulating them with it to further increase their power over them.

There isn't any certainty that this is an all-encompassing behavior personified and the possibility does exist that this reversed card may represent an isolated situation when one's emotions are being used against them to achieve a single objective. What is true with all reversed cards of the Court is that they are often a representation of an obstacle to progress, and the behaviors described by them may be a moment in time, or an ongoing behavior that will continue to affect one.

Another truth I will continue to express, is that the determination of which aspect is the one that fits the current situation comes from the context of the situation. There isn't anything the cards in a Tarot reading can clarify without the full participation of the one with the question.

Queen of Cups

UPRIGHT

Heartfelt is the primary descriptor for this card and it is the best adjective to describe any and all actions of someone for whom it is chosen to represent. They are the embodiment of good intentions, followed by the acts that fulfill those intentions. There are strong elements of loving and nurturing, as well as the instinctive or psychic awareness to know what is needed and when to apply it for the people for whom they care.

Possessing a mysterious quality that seems to be defined by *too good to be true*, this person or behavior is in fact not. Because their feelings truly emanate from the heart, they have a tendency to excel at artistic endeavors, as they can aptly bring what they feel into focus for others to see or hear. This is an easily recognizable person or trait as they are always the consummate good listener.

I have stated that the Court cards can represent people or a need to emulate associated behavior. It needs to be clearly stated as well that *emulate* is not meant as *imitate*, or *pretend*, but by definition to *equal* or *become* as this card describes. This card is genuine sincerity in every respect and there isn't any room for acting or pretense. If this card appears in a position associated with the person asking the question, it would be wise to evaluate how they see themselves in relation to how they project themselves.

Being able to feel and understand what others are feeling through their empathetic nature is another element that makes them an identifiable person. They are known to be very mature, sometimes beyond their years, and that allows this card to facilely defy an age classification system when depicting an individual.

There are some schools of thought that see the divisions of the four suits of the Court much like astrology in that certain behaviors are innate, and that defines you as *who* you are as a person. Without dismissing that entirely, the more viable approach is how we have learned to use the tools we are given.

The way to discover whether one is locked into behavioral patterns is to begin with empathy, or as the familiar cliché states, *put yourself in their shoes*. That is the main ingredient of being a caring and loving person and the very heart of this card. To think more about the well being of another more than oneself is a choice. Having decided that they were born that way, as in uncaring and selfish, is a rationalization of the choice not to, and since it veils the existence of a decision, it absolves them of the need to decide otherwise.

REVERSED

What can one do when they hold the heart of another in their hand? When this card appears reversed in a reading it won't be good. From infidelity to hidden agendas, there are deceptions in this situation, and there is no way to soften the likelihood of eventual heartbreak.

The elements that define this card reversed may seem obvious to others, but are completely unknown to the person with the greatest emotional stake. The ability to manipulate someone requires their trust in, and/or their dependency on, the one who would exploit it to realize their own personal goals, or achieve the self-gratification they desire. What makes this situation more tragic is the individual described in this card reversed is adept at identifying the vulnerable and trusting.

What should be obvious when this card appears reversed is that there will likely be two very distinct personalities involved in the situation, if it is of a romantic nature. One will be self-gratifying with secrets, and another with emotional weaknesses and gullibility that might easily be used and manipulated. The inevitable outcome here is, again, heartbreak.

When cracks appear, there may be at first denial by the one being used, in hopes that they are wrong, followed by empty promises by the other when they are eventually confronted. Whether it is a passive-aggressive approach or direct domination, it is truly the same in the end. Of course perceptions can play a significant role in the circumstances. Seeing what one wants and needs to see may perpetuate the situation by further empowering the other.

On the flipside, if one of the people involved is hypersensitive and emotionally unstable, their doubts may destroy a relationship that is real. With that revelation coming to light, this card reversed might seem perplexing. The truth about whether it is real or perceived lies in the heart of the person asking the question. Beginning with an honest and thorough self-examination, asking a specific question that allows the cards to provide an answer that can be recognized, and not denying the answer even if one does not like it, will lead to the truth.

If the relationship is not of a romantic nature, the essence of this card remains in the form of offered solutions under the guise of caring, and the exploitation of trust for self-gratification or personal gain.

King of Cups

UPRIGHT

This person is calm in any circumstances and they are always gracious, appreciative, kind, and considerate. One will feel sereneness in their presence, an omnipresent sincerity and warmth in everything about them.

Choosing this card to represent someone in readings has the drawback of possibly being done out of idealism, but by all means do so anyway. However, it is important to remember the difference between the perfect friend, lover, and partner depicted here, and those who are trying to be the best possible person. If one is sincerely attempting to be as this card describes, then they certainly qualify for this consideration.

They will always be conscientious of the feelings of anyone and everyone, and they do not find humor at the expense of others. Always forgiving and understanding as well, this person does not hold grudges, seek revenge, or even participate in recriminations.

Among the many elements described here are loyalty and trust, as they will keep any secret entrusted to them. These elements, combined with their compassion, and their ability to actively listen to others, make them very easy to confide in, and as well, their presence is comforting when one needs to talk about things that can be difficult to share – a person who always knows the right thing to say, and they also know when saying nothing is better. If one truly needs someone to be there for them, a person represented here is easily the best choice. They are tender, thoughtful, and romantic as a lover and partner, never selfish or self-gratifying.

The various elements that make up what this card personifies can be separated, and aside from choosing it as an individual representation, they can also apply to what one needs to draw from to be the person another needs one to be in the current situation. Each of us may be accurately defined by the attributes of the various Court members of a particular suit, but we are only limited by our choice to be consistent.

The interpretations of Court cards are always situational and perceptually dependent, and I am not describing a mask one should wear, but a sincerity of providing what is wanted or needed. Coincidentally, or perhaps not, this King is exactly the person who would see this and do just that for another.

REVERSED

If there were ever a time to spin positive the abilities of a confidence artist, it would surely be represented by this card found reversed. Toying with the emotions of others and exploiting another's love for personal gain is never a good thing, ever, but any person depicted here is at the top of that class.

Whether or not they have genuine feelings of their own is not determinable, and likely to be irrelevant, as they are a master at exploiting the vulnerabilities and weaknesses of others, with no mercy afforded. Unfortunately, it is hard to see them coming, and they will see through others with little or no difficulty. Just as all reversed Court cards can wear the mask of their upright counterparts, so to can this

King reversed, and the calling card here is thoughtful and romantic gestures used as bait.

Another element one might consider, is people who just can't take a hint and won't go away when something is over, or was never real in the first place. There may be unwanted and inappropriate expressions of love, including jealousy and possessiveness.

The obstacles presented here will play with emotions, as someone or a situation will be attempting to influence one to think with their heart instead of their head. Following one's heart is a good thing, but to do so without tempering decisions with input from the mind may have one in too deep before they realize what has happened. I consider myself to be a romantic, and I cherish the feeling of a genuine mutual love. Just because I write these words, I am no less susceptible to the possibility, as now I am being objective, otherwise, maybe not so much.

Characteristics that will be present here are infidelity and dishonesty, but combined with an indefinable ability to win one back and be forgiven. Eventually, the heart may weaken and the trust will dissipate, but how much one has invested in the relationship by that time can leave them committed to the possibility that each new chance one gives will provide different results.

Interpreting a reversed Court card such as this can be perplexing at times. One certainly doesn't want their love to be a tool or a weapon used against them, but at the same time to introduce suspicion into a genuine relationship can undermine it, and create a problem where one did not previously exist.

Page of Pentacles

UPRIGHT

A methodical and patient person or approach is described in the interpretation of this card. They will express an open fascination with nature, are adept in financial matters, and possess a thirst for knowledge of any discipline. There is a duality of natural things and financial matters inherent in the Pentacles suit, and on the surface, this could seem contradictory or conflicting, especially when referring to members of the Court. However, at the heart of this person or character trait is practicality and diligence, and the significance of being prepared for each step they take upon their path.

The ability to listen and express sincere interest in the intellectual opinions of others may often make them easy to recognize. For them there are few sources of information that are undeserving of consideration.

Anyone who tends a garden will easily relate to what is portrayed by the appearance of this card in a reading, or the designation of it as a Significator. The need to plan, research, and organize, in the interest of a successful garden is applicable to the beginning of any financial endeavor when expecting to realize the desired results. Along the way there is a need for frequent attention and necessary adjustments.

One of the strongest aspects of this card is preparation, and the person who is represented by this card understands that unanticipated possibilities leave too much to chance, and success is determined before they even take the first step. This easily translates into minimizing risk to the point where the path to their goal is almost always visible to them.

As I mentioned previously, the Pages are often Messengers, and the messages do not have limitations on their source or mode of travel. In the case of this Page, the messages will be in reference to matters involving finances, or possibly nature. It can actually be expanded to include aspects that define this card such as preparation and diligence.

Forming the basis of this card is the need to lay a foundation as one contemplates their goals and creates their expected path to achieve them. There are no actual restrictions to what those goals might be as the methodology described by this card can stand alone when this card appears in a reading.

REVERSED
There is a possibility of finding ineptitude in this card reversed, but it is much more common to find a lack of diligence and effort. Poor planning, a lack of attention to detail, and disorganization, due to a lack of effort or arrogance, are the staples of this interpretation. There are squandered opportunities, and financial ruin in the wake of the efforts of this person or the behavior described by this card. The ability to follow a path rests on knowing the path, and requires an understanding of what to expect and where to apply assets and resources. This is nearly if not completely absent here.

Clearly misunderstood here is that hopes and expectations are not the same thing. One is a matter of wanting something to happen, while the other is knowing why it should. From the gardening analogy, I can describe the difference in this card reversed as throwing seeds into the yard and hoping it will rain. There is very little if any planning, research, or organization on matters of preparation here.

Also included in the possible behaviors are the misappropriations of financial resources, whether with intent, or due to a failure to understand the consequences. It is unrealistic to believe that, under normal circumstances, someone would plan to fail, but they certainly can fail to plan. Even deeper into this card reversed one can find patterns of disregard and disrespect rooted in the arrogance of perceived entitlement. This can be even further exemplified by a lack of patience and condescension.

Let me remind you here that although it is not common practice to choose a reversed Court card as a Significator, there are no absolutes that one cannot. However, having said that, it does preclude the possibility of an important revealing in a reading, and the desire to do so may be driven by an emotional state that will have an effect on one's expectations.

Of the many aspects of this card, what applies in a reading can be a matter of what one can expect and avoid by heeding the possibilities if they pertain to the one the reading is for. Or it can initiate healthy skepticism if it refers to another entity.

Knight of Pentacles

UPRIGHT

Describing a very conscientious and dependable individual, this card represents the developmental stages of someone almost certainly on the path to success. It is important to realize that their definition of success is subjective, and is not always driven by materialistic ambitions. The behaviors one can easily recognize are patience and loyalty, in any situation. They are apt to be studious and will often excel academically, but by nature they see practical application as having greater value than theory.

Often moving slowly and methodically, they are at the same time relentless. This card depicts the personification of behaviors that are grounded and realistic, and they are the epitome of balance and temperament even in their youth. When choosing this card as a representation of someone, as is true with all Knights, and all members of the Court for that matter, it might be better to focus on the specific personality elements, not the gender.

With a strong affinity for animals and all life, they are very caring and self-sacrificing. They may apply these aspects and their relentlessness to causes that support animal rights, as well as the preservation of the Earth and its natural resources.

Among their strengths is the ability to anticipate and plan for events from a long-term perspective, in financial matters and all forms of goal setting. As I mentioned, the definition of success by the person depicted here is subjective, but they are not necessarily resistant to acquiring wealth and can be quite fond of luxury.

Of the Knights, these are the least prone to taking risks in all matters of love and finances. This does not define them as mistrusting, but instead patient enough to understand situations before they have invested themselves too deeply into them. They are often known to be quiet and unassuming, but this should not be attributed to shyness or insecurity. Instead, this person should be viewed as a contemplative and thoughtful observer.

As one might guess it may be easier to recognize this Knight by having eliminated the others as viable representatives of the individual you have in mind. Although this Knight will exhibit mature behavior, they are still considered to be young and the elements associated with them may appear at different levels of development.

REVERSED

The difference between the Pages and Knights reversed in any of the four suits can often be distinguished by age, as a simple interpretation. There are also developmental differences that should be considered as well. Starting with a lack of diligence and concern, the representation here may include a complete understanding of creating false expectations, and how they influence what is expected of someone. If one were disinclined to be involved in something, an expressed inability would likely allow them to avoid the responsibility of participation.

That brings to light one of the most important aspects of the behavior described here, and that would be irresponsibility. And that translates into somebody taking advantage of someone else in order to capitalize on a situation without effort. The lack of effort and due diligence can be attributed to laziness and/or feelings of entitlement, and this is recognizable in their smugness when they have successfully gained by the efforts of others.

There is apt to be greed, even fraud and thievery, which is rationalized under the guise of being owed, due to some prior and perceived unfair deal or feeling victimized. Quite unlike the upright interpretation of this card, when reversed there is often found a purely materialistic ambition, but again they seek to acquire through the efforts of others, not their own.

Another identifiable trait is their wide range of well-timed excuses. These can seem innocuous at first, but it shouldn't take long for them to pile up, and if the person being used does not revert to denial, then the behavior will eventually clarify the situation.

Irresponsibility and a lack of dependability are highlighted here, but not to the exclusion of avarice and ambition. Intentionally getting others to underestimate them in order to capitalize off the other's efforts, as opposed to their own, can be witnessed in alleged physical ailments or masquerading as incapable of specific skills.

As one might suspect, sympathy is a likely ploy and someone exhibiting this behavior will gladly take advantage of someone feeling sorry for them. In a close relationship, and under the right circumstances, they will employ emotional manipulation and blackmail to further their efforts toward their objectives through the actions of others. Their behaviors would be obvious if immediately displayed, so they will initially portray an illusion of hard work and diligence to ensnare those they desire to take actions for them.

Queen of Pentacles

UPRIGHT

The essence of practicality is found here, and although they may very well be a person of means and luxury, they are not frivolous, and do not act upon a whim. As a person, they are knowledgeable and make decisions based on research as well as an understanding of the implications to all possible outcomes. They are patient enough to build a foundation that will support and promote their future endeavors, and seldom move forward without a well thought-out plan to achieve their goals.

When faced with obstacles, they cannot be rushed, as they do not like to revisit past decisions and reevaluate the effects they might have had on their current situation. There isn't any presumptive behavior here, and they are willing to look for value in anyone's opinion.

What can make them easy to identify is their love of nature and extreme generosity toward causes associated with conservation. This isn't just in the form of monetary donations, as they will give physically of themselves to protect the environment as well. It shouldn't be surprising to find such a person tending their own garden, even if they have chosen to live on a large estate.

Their detail-oriented personality pushes them toward aesthetics, and, as a result, all things in their life are found to be clean and neat. The person represented by this card puts as much, if not more, value on the maintaining of things as they do in the acquirement of them. This applies to every aspect of their life, including relationships.

As an interpretation, one should consider a need to be practical and pay close attention to the things in life one cares about. It can also refer to a need to be thorough in preparing for an endeavor and taking situations more seriously.

Out of all the elements represented here, the one that stands out the most is the cherishing of all things, living and inanimate, tangible and intangible. They know what they want, they know how to get it, and they will do everything within reason to keep it, not only in their lives, but in the best condition possible. That it is invariably true for such a person represented here does not make it any less true for other members of the Court, but this really is a case of *what you see is what you get*.

REVERSED

This is often found to be the exact opposite of the upright interpretation for this card. If that doesn't seem simple enough, consider that this represents nothing but aesthetics – a hollow center to be specific. As a personification, they will lavishly spend money well beyond their means to appear affluent, while incurring debt they can't repay, even if they cared enough to try. They will measure others by their visible material wealth and attempt to form bonds with those who meet their perception, or expressed more accurately, misperception, of importance.

One can recognize elitism and snobbery, as well as a total lack of compassion and generosity in their behaviors. A tragic truth that one such person will live by is that anyone worth knowing would never need to ask for anything. You should easily see by now that normal social protocols such as politeness and gratitude are likely to be missing here.

As I have mentioned, a person more closely related to the reverse interpretation of a Court card can at times disguise themselves in the behaviors associated with the upright representation, and in this case, it is the show just for the sake of the show.

A person who would institute an elaborate high-ended con could easily be described by this card reversed, as the basis here is a lifestyle that is nothing more than a ruse to begin with. Whether they have a hidden agenda to gain from one or not, a person will quickly lose the ability to trust them as they are not known to be responsible or dependable in any situation. They may display an appreciation for nature, but it is more apt to be in the form of a country club, or a real estate investment scam.

A tendency to ally themselves with present company, and reflect the opinions of those they are currently speaking with, in order to serve their own personal interest or agenda will sooner or later become apparent. This element of their behavior defines their complete lack of loyalty to anyone other than themselves.

The obstacle one faces when this card appears reversed in a reading is truly a matter of perceptions, but it is likely to be affecting both sides of the situation—an intentional false projection spawned from perceived self-importance, and presented to influence the views of others as well as oneself.

King of Pentacles

UPRIGHT
Most often, this is the consummate businessperson, with the right plan, at the right place, at the right time. They are professional and methodical as they go about their work, and they fully understand that the most important part of any plan is the preparation. There is an element of sage advice found in this card, as it can represent a go-to person on how practical thinking can lead to success. One will not find any quick score, *get-rich-quick* schemes here, as the mentality is patience and diligence.

    As a representation of a person, look for them to be realistic, reliable, responsible, and honest, in all aspects of their lives. Success is calculated risk while maintaining a conservative foundation, and although the highs may not be extremely high, the lows will not be as devastating.

    The nature association with the suit of Pentacles will be evident through philanthropy and a business plan that is ethical and humane. This does not preclude material desires in one, and the attainment of wealth may actually be serving the greater purpose of generosity and charity toward causes that they feel are of great importance. This is also not to say that they do not enjoy luxury and the lifestyle wealth provides. What is found here is a healthy balance between having and giving to others.

The person this card describes will be thoughtful and receptive to not only the opinions, but the needs of others, and they are easily approachable. However, they are not known to take action without proper evaluation, and one will need patience in dealing with them.

It is necessary to keep in mind that success is relative to an individual, and a person who this card would represent may not have achieved success as others choose to view it, but in their mind, they have what they need and they live a high-quality life. That brings me to another significant element found in this card, and that is such a person will not judge others, especially on matters of material wealth.

I personally maintain the belief that every decision contains a practical, if not right choice. Perhaps described as conservative and safe, or safer at least, and if one always favors, if not chooses, that choice, they are the very person this card is likely to represent. An underlying possibility here is the consistency in the quality of life, not the stress of great risk, regardless of the potential reward.

REVERSED

Success built on a corrupt, dishonest, and an *anything goes, as long as I win* mindset, leads the possibilities here. The grand schemes of obtainment that are represented in this card reversed will not initially be obvious from a distance, as they will still display a methodical and patient approach. What will eventually stand out are their self-serving results; and as they achieve greater power, their actions will reveal their ruthlessness. If one finds themselves in a personal relationship with such a person, their licentious behaviors will become visible far more rapidly. This is a result of their propensity to boast about their plans, flexing their diabolical intellectual muscles if you will, and they will seek to establish a relationship with someone they feel will admire them.

When encountering an obstacle that might be depicted here, one should expect attempts to create a sense of obligation that compromises and diverts progress away from one's own goals. There will be deals made in bad faith, where one will find their trust exploited in the hopes of drawing one in and catching them off guard.

The biggest difficulty one may face is the apparent lack of alternatives in the current situation. It isn't that there is not a right choice to be made, but the situation may have been engineered to put one at odds with their own progress, and making the choice they wish to make will bring with it greater conflict. What this commonly relates to is someone getting ahead by pushing others down, or creating situations where others inadvertently self-sabotage their own efforts. Everything in this card reversed points toward inappropriately achieved success, or attempts to manipulate others for one's own personal gain. It should be interpreted primarily in regards to material and financial gain using undue influence and deceptive and corruptive means.

Since this in fact is a King, it is not likely to be representative of a petty thief, but one should not rule out thievery entirely. Such things as con games and embezzlement, or even extortion and blackmail, could be possible here. I believe, in this case, the word *respect* would be a bad choice, but one must give this King reversed their due, as they are not inept or insufficient mentally to achieve financial success; they simply have no moral or ethical foundation and thrive just as much on the failures of others as they do their own successes.

Tarot Spreads

To get the most out of your Tarot cards, they should be placed and viewed in a layout known as a spread. This is the process known as a Tarot reading. The places in the spread known as positions are predefined in order to describe people, circumstances, events, and outcomes in situations one may wish to inquire about for greater enlightenment.

There are spreads of all types, with some specific to love and relationships, and others for creativity or other endeavors. I couldn't possibly list them all here, but I will provide a few and describe how to read with them.

TAROT SPREADS

Three Card

This is a simple reading for determining:

- Where you are,
- How you got there, and
- Where you are going.

Choose a Significator, if you wish to include one, before shuffling and lay it face up on a surface. If you have a specific question to ask, formulate it while shuffling.

At this point, you have a choice between fanning the cards face down, and drawing three random cards, or pulling the top three cards as you hold the deck face down in your hand.

CARD 1

Either way, the first card should be placed face down half covering the Significator if one was selected, and **this represents the present or current situation**.

CARD 2

The second card should be placed face down to the left of the first card **to represent how you arrived at the current situation**.

CARD 3

Then place the third card face down to the right of the first card. This represents **where the current situation will lead.**

Now turn over the cards in the order you placed them: center, left, then right. If reading reversals, be sure to turn the cards from side to side, not top to bottom or bottom to top, as this will make sure that the cards remain upright or reversed as you placed them.

Then interpret in the same order: center, left, and then right. Again, this represents where you are, how you got there, and where you are headed. This spread can respond to any question for which you wish to find an answer.

Celtic Cross

This is easily the most popular multi-card Tarot spread, and can be utilized to answer any question, on any situation, that you may find yourself wishing to inquire about.

Choose a Significator if you want one, shuffle the cards and think of your question, then say it aloud as you place the cards in their positions.

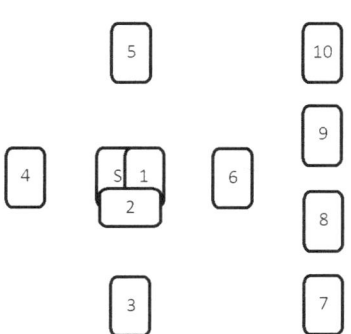

S – SIGNIFICATOR

A specific card usually chosen from the sixteen Court cards to **represent someone a question is about**.

1ST POSITION

This is you in the current situation, if you are reading for yourself. If reading for someone else, then obviously it represents him or her.

2ND POSITION

Representing a positive or negative influence in the current situation, this is known as the Crossing Card.

3RD POSITION

The situation the reading is about will have a prompting event or person who will lead to the question you have chosen to ask the cards. This is sometimes called the catalyst position.

4TH POSITION

Here is the **position of the past**, and it describes previous elements that relate to the current situation. Sometimes referred to as recent past, but that aspect is relative, and there are not any absolutes.

5TH POSITION

Known as the Crowning Card, this position is reflective of your **ideals or expectations**, but also has the ability to describe disillusionment or misplaced priorities.

6TH POSITION

A point in time in the **near future** where a person or event will create a decision you will need to make that will influence the outcome of the situation.

7TH POSITION

This is known as the self-image position, and will describe **how one thinks and feels in the current situation**. It has the ability to reveal denial, if you are actually paying attention.

8TH POSITION

Your environment and the people around you can influence the situation, and this position represents **the role outside forces will play** in the matter at hand.

9TH POSITION

What you hope for, or what you fear from the current situation, will often be displayed here. It can also depict someone or something unexpected coming into play.

10TH POSITION

Here you have the **outcome** position, which will display the results of your current course of progress, barring a dramatic altering of intentions or efforts.

Vincit Omnia Veritas

This is an original spread that I created for self-evaluation, and the name translates to *Truth Conquers All*. Its purpose is to foster honesty in evaluating the situation, but more importantly, in oneself.

- There is not an applied question for this reading, so just clear your mind.
- Separate the cards by the four suits including the Court cards, and leave the Major Arcana in a separate pile.
- Shuffle each of the five stacks of cards.
- When placing the cards in their positions, do so face down without looking at them. I will explain further in Doing a Reading, and here I will describe the positions and refer you to the diagram.

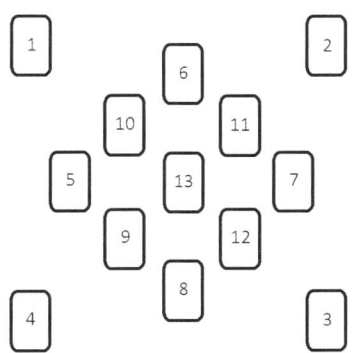

1ST POSITION

This represents **your thoughts or conscious awareness**, so draw a card from the Sword pile and place it here.

2ND POSITION

Pull a card from the Wands stack and place it here, as this is **your passion, drive, or desire**.

3RD POSITION

In this position, place a card from your stack of Pentacles, and this will represent **the material aspect of your life.**

4TH POSITION

From your pile of Cups, draw a card and place it in this position to describe **the way you feel, as in emotions, perhaps love.**

5TH POSITION

This is **a bridge**, so place a card from your Major Arcana stack.

6TH POSITION

This is **a bridge**, so place a card from your Major Arcana stack.

7TH POSITION

This is **a bridge**, so place a card from your Major Arcana stack.

8TH POSITION

This is **a bridge**, so place a card from your Major Arcana stack.

At this point put all five piles together, and thoroughly shuffle all the remaining cards from the deck.

Now place cards from all of the remaining in the following positions.

9TH POSITION

Place a card here from the remaining cards as your **emotions connecter.**

10TH POSITION

Place a card here from the remaining cards as your **thought connecter.**

11TH POSITION

Place a card here from the remaining cards as your **passion connecter.**

12TH POSITION

Place a card here from the remaining cards as your **material connecter.**

13TH POSITION

This is **your present state or destination** as the four elements converge.

For more on using this spread see the Doing a Reading section.

Doing a Reading with the Vincit Omnia Veritas

Within this text, I have made numerous references to perceptions and expectations, and I believe they are the true indicator of who we are, which subsequently leads to where we are in our lives. Each of us actually carries around three distinct perceptions that encompass ourselves and the others we interact with.

First, there is how we see ourselves as a person, and second, there is how we want others to see us. We have a propensity to create a projected image of ourselves that keeps certain aspects somewhat secret within the thoughts of our mind, at the very least, and this projection differs from what we actually understand about ourselves. This is not to say that we all have a secret dark side, but actually just aspects of our personalities we do not intentionally reveal. The third perception belongs exclusively to others and consists of how they actually *do* perceive you. This is a blend of the first two and also includes elements from their own personality based on what experiences they have had in their own life.

A person only has control over the third perception by fully understanding the first two and why they are different. It stands to reason that most of us want others to think well of us, and in that regard, the second perception, the projected one, may represent an ideal, and this would infer the intent to become the projected image. Of course this depends on whether a person has a hidden agenda and is attempting to influence a person toward a decision they would not normally make.

I designed this Tarot spread for the purpose of self-evaluation and you should not choose a Significator for yourself when using it, as it is highly likely, if not a certainty, that it will reflect the projected image of oneself. There also is no need for a question because it is standardized to *who am I right now?* It is slightly complex, but the greatest difficulty lies in your ability to be honest with yourself.

After having separated the deck into five individual piles, the four complete suits and the Major Arcana, shuffle each pile thoroughly. Now place the thirteen cards face down in their respective places as described in the diagram. Remember to follow the steps I described in the prior chapter to make sure the cards in each position are drawn from the correct grouping of cards. Turn the cards face up, left to right or right to left to maintain reversal integrity, in the same order they were placed into the spread.

FIRST POSITION

Looking at the card in the First Position, you will see one of the fourteen possible Swords. This is the position of conscious thought and intent, and reflects the flow of your thoughts. It describes where you think you are now based on where you have been and where you think you are going, with the latter defining intent.

SECOND POSITION

In the Second Position there will be a Wand, which will represent someone or something of passion, or what you feel strongly about. It is important to stay focused in the moment, and although this card can represent a lifelong dream, it might not be what you feel the strongest about right now.

THIRD POSITION

The Third Position is money and the material as represented by the suit of Pentacles. This does not describe what you project about your current financial situation, but how it actually has evolved up until now, and how that relates to the future.

FOURTH POSITION

A card from the suit of Cups will represent your feelings and emotions in the Fourth Position. Different than desire or thoughts, emotions are reactions to situations that occur, and this can also describe love, where just the presence of someone can generate a feeling. When you encounter someone or something that you desire or have been thinking about, you will experience emotions that signify its presence.

FIFTH POSITION

The Fifth Position is a bridge between your thoughts and emotions and is described by a card from the Major Arcana. This can flow in either direction, and the complexity of interpreting the card here is removed by being honest with yourself. What do you feel that makes you think this way, or what are you thinking that makes you feel a certain way?

SIXTH POSITION

Another Major Arcana card will make the bridge between thoughts and passions, and is found in the Sixth Position. The connection between how your passions drive your thoughts or intentions, or how what you think sparks your strongest desire, is what will be revealed by the card that appears in this position.

SEVENTH POSITION

In the Seventh Position is how passionate you are about material things, or the inverse, to what degree your material or financial state drives your passions and desires. This bridge, indicated by a card from the Major Arcana, describes how what you have affects what you strongly want to do, or how strongly you are driven towards the material.

EIGHTH POSITION

The relationship between your feelings and the material is depicted in this bridge represented by a Major Arcana card in the Eighth Position. Obviously, this is how you feel about money and what it can provide, or how material things affect your emotions. One way to view this bridge is to consider the elements of comfort and security.

NINTH POSITION

Connecting you and your emotions is the Ninth Position, and this card placed from all of the remaining cards in the deck, flows toward your current state, or destiny, in the center of the spread. This card represents how who or what you care about or love affects who you are in your life right now.

TENTH POSITION

Your thoughts are connected to your current state or destiny via the Tenth Position card, and the flow is inward toward you, in the center of the spread. What you think about, and how you think about it, represents who you are since they play, or should play, a strong role in your decision making.

ELEVENTH POSITION

How your passions define you in your current state is the Eleventh Position connector, and this drives you to be who you are right now. Flowing toward the center card that represents your current state or destiny, this position is what might be described as someone or something you live for, now or in the future.

TWELFTH POSITION

Found in the Twelfth Position is the way money and material things connect to how your life is now, or to your destiny. Once again, the connectors like this one flow toward the center of the spread. It can reflect practical thinking in your current situation, or how you are building future financial security. It could also describe how you are not doing well on matters of money and the material.

THIRTEENTH POSITION

The Thirteenth Position is you in your current state with all the elements combined. As I mentioned, this may also represent your destiny, and determining whether it represents now, or a time in the future, is actually the best way to figure out what is between where you are now, and where you want to be in your life.

Notes on the Vincit Omnia Veritas

The more you work with this spread, the better you should understand yourself, and the obstacles that stand in your way.

You will notice when reading with the *Vincit Omnia Veritas* spread, that both the bridges and connectors will often simultaneously work in both directions. What you should come to be cognizant of are the things you know, but don't think about, and why you think about the things you do not know about.

The *Vincit Omnia Veritas* spread is not designed to answer questions about love and money; there are plenty of other spreads that will serve those purposes, but instead, it should help you get more out of the other spreads by generating self-evaluation.

The truth of who you are is the only place you can start. If you don't know why you ask a question, you will have a difficult time recognizing and understanding the answers you receive. Seek the truth in yourself, through honest evaluation, and you will conquer the obstacles that stand in your way and realize your destiny.

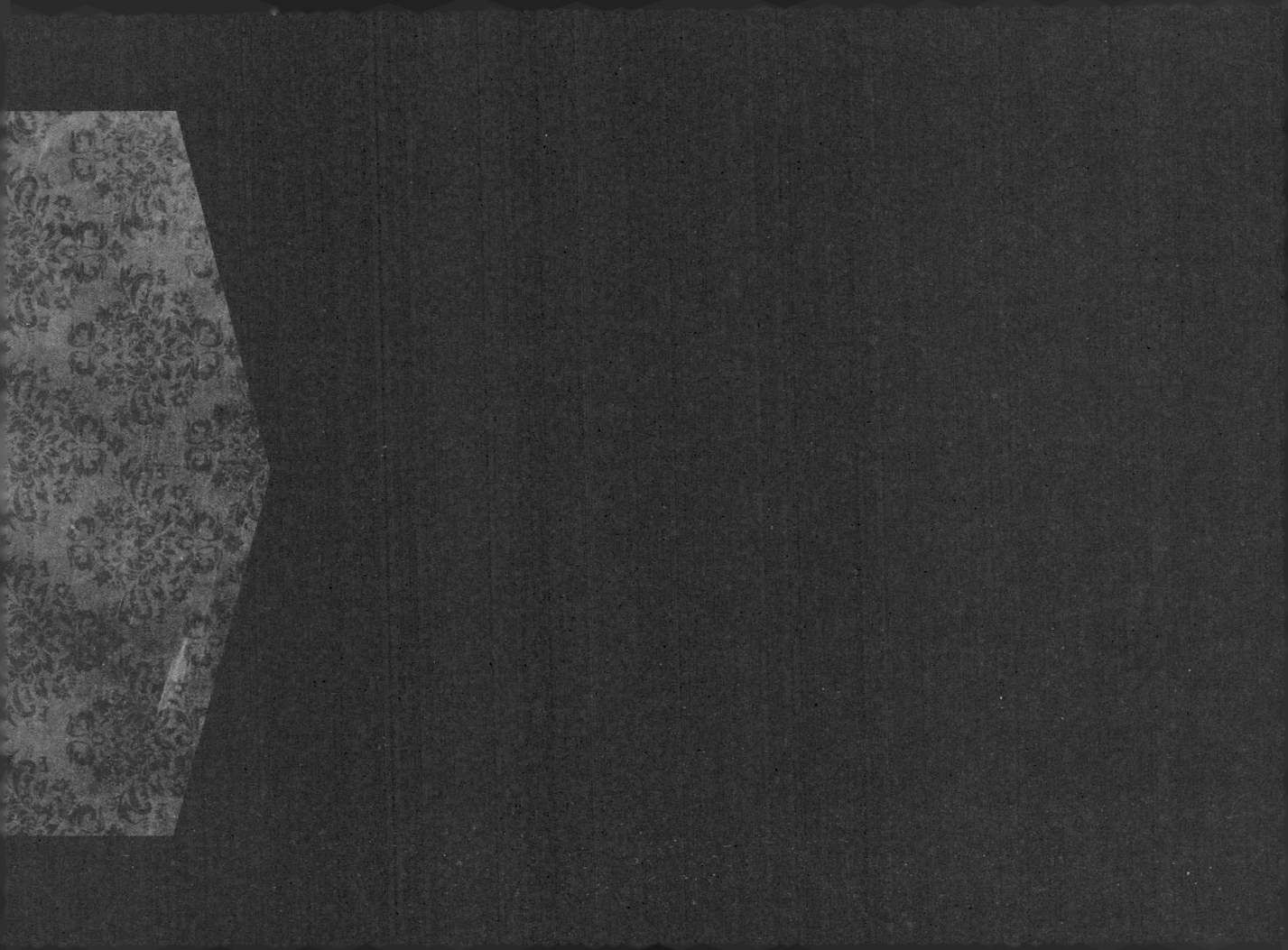

When all is
said and done

Tarot is a passionate embrace between the have and the hope. It is where life finds love and becomes the love of a lifetime. To *think* that something is possible is to *know* it is possible, and this takes only one's faith in the very reason one has the ability to think of what they should have in their life.

What are dreams, those strange vignettes that play out in our heads that we can't figure out when we wake up in the morning? Okay, so they are strange, but why can we see situations in our head that do not exist? And better yet, why can we manipulate them into a virtual reality when we are awake, where we can feel true love, passion, success, and an idealistic place where anything we want can be ours?

The previous questions do not need to be answered; they are intended to prompt you to think about the gift, the actual power you have to envision what you want in life, and how that allows you to define a path to realization.

The Tarot cards won't get you there; you will, but insight into possibilities is a valuable tool if it is properly applied. If you want to get the most out of a Tarot reading, you cannot hope to see your dreams come true in the cards that lay about before you; that is the same as the dream that is in your head.

It would be unrealistic to believe that *nothing will stand in your way*, but if you add just a little bit to that sentence, and make it *nothing will stand in your way that you are not ready to face and overcome*, then you have the point and purpose of the Tarot.

Finding cards in a reading that do not interpret as a positive is an advantage that can make a difference, but that depends on how the cards affect your perceptions and expectations. Things that you don't want to happen will happen – you know that, and you really don't need me to tell you that – but what I am telling you is that it is you, not the cards, that will determine your destiny. The Tarot cards are only what you take away from them, nothing more.